Tyranny of the Common Man

and

The Perversion of American Liberties

by Ralph Cantafio, M.D.

Publishing Rights: Turner Publishing Company
This book or any part thereof may not be reproduced
without the written consent of the author and publisher.

Turner Publishing Company Staff:
Publishing Consultant: Douglas W. Sikes

Library of Congress Catalog Card No. 98-89663

ISBN: 978-1-68162-154-8

Additional copies may be purchased directly from the publisher.
Limited Edition.

Chapter Index

ABOUT THE AUTHOR

Doctor Ralph Cantafio was born in Philadelphia, Pennsylvania and attended Ursinus College and Jefferson Medical College. He practiced a number of years as a General Practitioner. In the days when Medicine was a calling rather than a business, the family doctor was often considered a member of the family. Because of this position, the General Practitioners were intimately involved with family relations.

From the time that he was a young man, Ralph has been a student of modern history and the political sciences. The combination of his extensive experience in family relationships and his other interests, made him an eyewitness to the effect of one upon the other. The great changes which have occurred in American society the last twenty years, as a result of political, ethical and moral change, has had a profound effect upon our lives. Since Ralph has always had an interest in the literary art, he now has turned his experiences and observations into a book. He has done this in order to make the public aware of the forces that have turned American society away from the path as envisioned by our forefathers.

PREFACE

Since mankind first ascended from the primeval tribes, it was their destiny to live generation after generation subjected to the domination and tyranny of others. As tribes formed communities and communities towns, cities and nations, the masses were ruled by those who were strong enough to grasp and hold the reigns of power. First came the kings and the emperors and then, "The Greats," the Pharaohs and the Khans, then Potentates and the "Exalted Ones." All of these ruled by decree or whim and had absolute power over the lives and deaths of their subjects. However, somewhere within the human breast was a constant whisper inciting the human spirit to break its bonds. Finally this small voice was at long last heard in the land of the Greeks, and the first government in which the average person had some say in their destiny was created. As the Greek Empire rose and fell, the freedom of the human spirit peaked and waned with it; to be rekindled again by the glory that was Rome. During the existence of the Roman Empire some semblance of mankind directing their own destiny was again achieved with varying degree of success. Throughout the establishing of world domination by the armies of Rome, the Pax Romano which followed, and its final decline and fall, varied degrees of freedom were allowed selected citizens of Rome. Nevertheless, even during these early experimentations, true individual freedom guaranteed to every citizen of a nation had not been totally achieved.

With the eventual fall of the Roman Empire, gradually came the Dark Ages. During that period of history, whatever advances was made in personal freedoms were totally lost and the masses were turned into serfs, again subject to the whims and demeanor of their lords and national leaders. Mankind seethed under the yolk of injustice and suppression and yearned for the day when that spirit of self expression and freedom within them would once again be allowed to surface.

In western civilization this spark finally manifested itself in the signing of the Magna Carta in Runnymede, England in 1215 by King John under the compulsion of his barons. This gradually led to some loosening of the regal grasp upon the lives and aspirations of the common masses. With the discovery of the New World, the human race finally had its first chance at establishing a social system completely unhindered by the traditions of the past. This led to the establishment of colonies on the continent of North America, and finally to a confrontation between ruler and those who wished to guide their own destinies. The American Revolutionary War for independence finally severed the chain to those who would carry their repressive malevolence to a new unspoiled world. Once the British were defeated, the last obstacle to a truly free and independent people was at last overcome. For the first time in the history of the world, a nation of truly free people was finally established on God's earth. Freedom at last! The aspirations of the human race, since mankind first was able to comprehend their own true worth, had at long last been realized.

The human spirit had been released from bondage and like the American eagle, the symbol of this new nation, soared unshackled in all directions. The Declaration of Independence had started the process, the Bill of Rights had spelled out in uncompromising terms those freedoms which are the birth right of all human beings, and the Constitution had sealed forever a covenant between this new government and its people.

At last, in America there was established what all men had yearned for from the beginning of time; to be a citizen of a nation in which the people governed themselves. No more Monarchs! No more Emperors! No more oppression! No more tyranny! In this new nation citizens would govern themselves to insure that the dignity of the human spirit would never again be trampled upon. There would be liberty in this new nation. Life, liberty and the pursuit of happiness, but most important of all, LIBERTY!

As a small agrarian nation of God fearing people of high morals who aspired to further the cause of civilization, the United States of America prospered and became everything that the founding fathers had hoped for. This had genuinely become a nation without tyranny.

As the fledgling nation grew, however, and the dawn of the industrial revolution was about to rise upon it, social structures were beginning to change. Before these changes could produce a demonstrable altering of the public demeanor, the United States were thrown into the agony of civil war. This war itself caused such a distortion of national priorities that any change in social values was hardly discernible. However, like all things, the war finally came to and end. Once the nation had gotten over the political chaos following the assassination of President Lincoln and the embarrassment of reconstruction, this nation was ready to go forward again. Gradually the full potential of American resources, both in raw materials and its people, was being realized. Consequently, The United States of America, in spite of a great depression and two greater wars, developed into a mighty industrial nation and became the most prosperous and powerful country on earth.

This, however, was not accomplished without a price. The wages that this nation was to pay for its achievements was of far greater cost than mere monetary compensation. It was even greater than that paid by those courageous men who died or were wounded on many foreign battlefields. The price this nation paid was the loss of its basic values. For a democratic society that was based on the love of God, country and family to lose these values, was the highest price of all!

The United States of America was created as a Christian nation. Although freedom of religion was guaranteed to all, this country's basic principles were based on Christian doctrines and beliefs. The moral foundations of this democracy were based on the Ten Commandments, and the oath to swear to uphold the Constitution of this great nation was based on the belief and fear in God. This did not evolve because of any prejudice towards the belief of others, but because of our forefather's unshakable opinion that a democratic process cannot exist without a solid moral basis. For a democracy to function its people must first have good will towards their neighbors and others in the community. They must put the welfare of the nation and the majority before their own. They must be people who abhor injustice and believe in the orderly process of law. They must be citizens who believe that bearing false witness against anyone is a crime against God. They must believe that immorality will weaken the fibers of righteousness and lead to the compromising of those who must elect, and those who must serve, in the government of a society which governs themselves. Therefore, our founding fathers based this government on the highest authority that they knew and believed would sustain the institutions of this new nation; Christianity. Democracy can only be the offspring of good, not of evil. Totalitarian governments are based on cruelty and the denying of all basic human rights. They have as their basis the belief that only the strong should rule, and that its citizens have allegiance to no other authority figure, on earth or in heaven, than their national leader. Their laws are not based on truths, but on lies and distortions. This nation's founding fathers recognized this fact, and therefore, founded this nation on the greatest good and truth they knew; the Bible and the belief in a supreme being as described and explained by Jesus Christ. One must remember that the creators of this nation came from a Christian society. Also, that the early development of this country and the origination and practical development of its institutions were under Christian tutorship. During those periods, the majority of this new nation's citizens were of the Protestant Denomination with a few Catholics and those of the Jewish faith interspersed. Therefore, it was fitting and understandable that the creation of The United States of America was based on the religion which to these early Americans represented their highest aspirations. They certainly would not entrust the moral integrity of this free society on those who did not believe in God, or to those whose religions were based on vengeance or lack of good will towards others. The reason that democracy was given a religious basis, was to insure the integrity of its institutions by perpetuating its continuity into the hands of those whose motives would be based on moral principles that would insure honest government and protect the liberty of its citizens. The desire of our founding fathers to separate church and state was not to undermine the Christian basis of its government, but to insure that full freedom of religion was given to its citizens, trusting in the belief that those who governed this country would be chosen by a majority who would elect only God fearing men and women.

This religious moral foundation helped create a society that was based on the principles of trust in God and the golden rule. Consequently, this country became a nation of order and propriety. Its citizens demonstrated respect for the elderly, authority and the law, as well as reverence for its religious institutions and admiration and appreciation for the learned and their academic institutions. The United States of America was a good neighbor and a model for those societies who craved orderliness and decency as well as liberty.

This nation, that was carved out of a virgin land, had the opportunity to plan and build new cities unencumbered by old communities of the past. In the northeast the largest of well planned cities were developed. Without old buildings to first tear down and plenty of available land, American and European architects unleashed their skills and imaginations as they built beautiful cities with large boulevards and stately buildings. Parks were developed and municipal buildings were erected as well as townhouses. Many cities became not only the place for commercialism, culture, churches and commerce, but also for homes; this time not only for the gentry, but also for the common man. Most cities had a main street and off of these other secondary streets ran in different patterns. These streets contained the large commercial and municipal buildings, the Museums, Theaters, Opera Houses, Music Houses, saloons and restaurants. Surrounding this area, which acquired the name of, "Downtown," were street after street of privately owned homes. An entire street of homes was called a block and blocks were divided by streets and alleys. The types of houses varied according to neighborhood, city or geographic location. There were single homes, semi-detached homes, twin homes and row homes. Multiple dwellings were the apartments, flats or boarding houses. Some people rented their dwellings and others bought them. Regardless of which, most took special pride in the appearance of the place where they lived. The brass kick plates, doorknobs, door plates and push plates were always polished and shiny. The marble fronts and steps on those houses that had them, were constantly scrubbed by the domestics, or proud owners, to keep them scrupulously clean. It was not unusual on a Saturday morning to see rows of women in each block scrubbing these marble steps and fronts.

Some cities were characterized by these practices, and even today we still hear about the white steps of Baltimore. The pavements in front of each house was kept clean by the resident who swept them frequently with a broom. Although the sanitation departments periodically swept and washed the streets, frequently the gutter in front of the house was not clean enough for the occupant and it was in addition hosed down and swept by someone who lived in the house. In fact, it was not unusual for people who lived in a block to call the street department to ask them to turn on the fire hydrant, so they could form a broom brigade and clean the entire gutter.

This new nation, up until World War II, was known for not only its clean cities, but also for its freedom from street crime and burglary. People, when not at home, frequently put their key to the front door under the door mat. They slept on hot summer nights with the doors open and the screen doors latched only by a hook and eye to hold them closed. Public phone books remained for years in the phone booths of the local drugstores, train and bus stations. Although they were bleached and discolored by the sun and dog eared, they were seldom defaced or destroyed. Public toilets, although always a target for wall graffiti, were usually clean and well maintained. Few would tear tissue holders off the wall vandalize these facilities to the extent that they had to be closed or abandoned in desperation.

The large cities were established during a period in the American economy when the ownership of motorized transportation was not possible for everyone. Therefore, first using horsepower and then putting the new energy source of electricity to use, fast, cheap, public transportation was developed. First came the street cars (called trolleys), and then the elevators and the subways, criss-crossing these large cities, making the ability for people to go to work and shop and travel an inexpensive and readily available commodity. In good weather or bad, in driving rain or blizzard, in the scorching heat of summer or the pleasant days in spring, public transportation like some perpetual motion machine was always in operation to bring the public to their appointed destinations. Public transportation was clean and efficient, with courteous conductors and motormen to speed the public on its way and call out the stops before these giant conveyors of human cargo ground to a screeching halt. Inside these carriers, the seats were intact and the floors and walls were clean. The walls above the seats were lined with unmolested colorful advertisements neatly framed by shiny chrome strips. Clearly displayed on the first panel was a permanently placed enameled sign which announced that it was illegal to smoke, spit, or talk to the motormen while the transport was in motion.

As The United States grew and territories became States, the new cities of the Midwest and West were modeled after these glittering cities of the Northeast. The South, slow to recover from its war with the North and less willing to change its established traditions, followed initially a more or less different course.

During the late 1920s and early 1930s, the large number of immigrants and the migration of minorities from the South produced slums and brought crime to the Northeastern cities. However, most of the residential areas, except during the era of Prohibition, were relatively free of crime and the blighted areas represented a very small part of the large sprawling cities. America was still clean, orderly and beautiful.

The American dream was being realized by many citizens of this new democracy, as the growing industries produced many jobs which in turn generated a public which could pay for many of the services previously afforded only by the wealthy. Most Americans were glad to have a job and were courteous and conscientious workers. An honest days work for fair pay, seemed to be this new country's creed. The work ethics of this early period were already established as traditional values brought to America by the early settlers and new immigrants. Bakers arose in the wee hours of the morning to bake bread, and the milkman and breadman had delivered their wares long before the public arose in the morning. Doctors made house calls, and pharmacies closed late at night and opened early in the morning. Trolleys, elevators and subways ran on time, unless bad weather or an accident delayed them. Craftsman arrived when they promised and were courteous as they did their jobs with skill and pride in their work. The Great Depression caused great suffering and fear in the hearts of those who experienced it and produced an animosity in the blue collar work force not easily forgotten.

Up until World War II, married women with children were primarily mothers and wives. Their offspring were children until they were adults. The family unit was the basis of American society and mothers saw to its welfare and comfort while the fathers provided for its support and protection. It was not demeaning for a woman to be a housewife and mother, nor was the father considered a chauvinist if he wished to provide for his family without the assistance of his wife. In fact, it was a source of pride for a family to have a father and husband who could provide for all of them without added assistance. Women preferred mates who had the potential to be good providers and men looked for women who had the qualities that would make good mothers and wives.

Children were considered to be children until they became adults. There was no separate classification called teenager or adolescent. Adolescence was a physiological stage that children went through on their way to becoming adults and did not give them any particular status or privileges. Idleness was considered to be the devil's playtime and all children were given chores to do at home. Many were encouraged by their parents to find part-time jobs to fill their idle hours. Children were raised to respect their parents, authority and the elderly, as well as the property of their neighbors and others. Their lives were carefully structured. They arose in the morning, ate breakfast and departed for school. When they arrived home after school they found their mothers anxiously awaiting their return. They did their chores and then went out to play. Children had to be home in time for supper. The entire family ate this meal together and no one was excused from the table until supper was over. On weekdays, the children next did their homework, and if they finished in time could listen to the radio until it was bedtime, which was early by today's standards. Saturdays was reserved for major chores and for leisure time with friends or family, if the child did not work. On Sunday, the entire family went to church and then had Sunday dinner, which was the most elaborate and special meal of the week. Frequently relatives or friends were invited for Sunday dinner which was a must for the recently married offspring.

In this way discipline was maintained under the ever present eye of the parents with guidance and love. This system worked admirably for generations of Americans and produced citizens of excellent character who were good students, informed adults and well adjusted parents.

The public attitude concerning crime during that period was that every person was responsible for their own actions. The majority of people believed that unless a person accused of a crime was found mentally afflicted, when the accused was found guilty by their peers, they should suffer the full penalty of the law befitting their crimes. Society did not take upon itself the blame for the actions of others. They held that every human being was accountable for their own actions to the laws of the land and to God. The public believed that incarceration was primarily for punishment and that anyone who with premeditation took the life of another should forfeit their own under a legal sentence of death. Abortion as well as rape were believed to be heinous and unspeakable crimes.

During this same period in American history, the moral fiber of the family was jealously guarded by the parents. Although historians may call this, "the Victorian mentality," of early America, one would find that this was more a belief fostered by the strong convictions of Christianity and would have flourished in America even if Queen Victoria had never sat on the English throne. Obscenities were considered to be vulgar and the product of undisciplined minds. They were not tolerated by the family unit and many mouths were washed out with soap for their utterance in anger or frustration. The use of foul language in front of a child or woman was considered to be a boorish act and a sign of ignorance and disrespect. This frequently led to sever physical retaliation on the perpetrator from the nearest concerned male. Although pornography was recognized as an ever present temptation to young people with the usual sexual curiosity, those who peddled it were considered to be perverted and deranged and were shunned by society and shown no mercy by the law.

Pornography among adults was a different matter. It was considered to be degrading, beneath ones self-respect and to diminish the esteem that others held for those engaged in viewing such material. These preoccupations caused a person's morality to be questioned and made them suspect as to their designs on the opposite sex and children. These practices were also condemned, because they made women appear as objects to be used, rather than loved and respected.

Immodesty was considered to be the forerunner of immorality. As men and women matured, they recognized that the lost of modesty, in either sexes, only led to the breakdown in other values which would eventually lead to the acceptance as commonplace those acts which heretofore were considered taboo.

As the young United States of America reveled in its innocence and new found prosperity, more than war clouds were forming on its horizon. This nation of the free; this land of liberty with justice for all, was to experience a new kind of tyranny. It was not to be fostered by the loss of freedom or suppression by a higher authority, but by the perversion of its own liberties by a new tyranny never before present in human society; the tyranny of the common man! Its affect would be more far reaching and as equally destructive, as that provided by a Nero or a despotic king of the middle ages. All those basic values held so dear by the American people, would be altered by a new generation who in their arrogance would betray those principles which made this nation the greatest moral force on earth.

CHAPTER I

When those who yearned for freedom were in bondage, they envisioned a time in which the human race would be free and in charge of their own destiny. This, they were certain, would create a society of just and law biding people. They were equally certain, that a free society would have citizens who would respect the opinions of others and would do naught to interfere with individual freedoms. It was innately believed that the common man was good and those who oppressed them were evil. There was never any doubt, in any of their minds, that the ills of the world were the result of ruthless despots and their underling who insured their rule by force. It was fervently believed that once these despots and those who kept them in power were gone, that the world would then lose most of its injustices, oppression and lawlessness.

When the world experienced its first true democracy, the founders of this nation's form of government did so on the assumption that this generally held opinion was true. Those who created the government of the United States of America founded it on the major premises that people of good will should be governed by a system of laws rather than men. All the rights of the citizens of this new nation would be spelled out in articles and bills. In order that these rights would never be abridged they were to be protected and guaranteed by laws. The rights of its citizens were written down in clear precise language so that they could never be denied or circumvented. The Constitution and The Bill of Rights were exact written instruments of these rights that guaranteed this nation's liberties forever. Life was given to its citizens by their creator, the pursuit of happiness was the prerogative of the individual, but liberty was given and warranted to them by the Constitution of The United States of America. With full knowledge that not all members of the human race are noble and pure, the founding fathers and legions of members of the judicial system to come, formulated laws to protect its citizens and punish the guilty. Then fearful that the laws would be too rigid and to protect the innocent from entrapment, they created exceptions and rights of appeal. All this was done so that no law would violate the rights of its citizens guaranteed under the Constitution. The purpose of this careful structuring of the laws was so that the innocent didn't have any reason to fear them and the guilty would be sure to be punished. The liberties of this nation were to be upheld and protected by the President, the Congress and the Supreme Court of The United States of America.

The careful planning of our founding fathers, however, overlooked one chink in the armor it had provided to protect this country's liberties. They never even envisioned that within the common man also lurked their own brand of tyranny. They never considered the possibility that the liberties that they insured could ever be denied or circumvented, could be perverted. In the act of corruption, those who are charged with the dispensing of the law and the protection of the liberties of others, lose their integrity and with their loss of honor succumb to the temptation of bribes or to compromise. They in fact break the law themselves in seeking to change the established judicial or elected outcome. In the act of perversion, citizens overextend the original meaning of those rights and liberties guaranteed them by the law, to alter their original purpose. In effect, they are over liberalizing the laws and rights of this nation to the extent that they no longer produce the results that they were originally intended. Those opinions that make individuals members of the liberal philosophy are not what undermines our system, it is the over liberalization of our basic rights that exceeds the bounds of reason which prevents liberty.

Unfortunately, in the process of developing this true democracy, one unexpected revelation that came to light was that tyranny lay not only in the souls of kings and dictators, but was also built into the fibers of the common man. Now that ordinary men and women were free to follow their own destinies, they were not all filled with the milk of human kindness. The rewards of capitalism lured many of these totally free citizens to prey upon their countrymen. Armed with the new weapon of wealth they set about to enslave others economically. Many used every unfair practice available to take advantage of those who sought only to work and provide for their families. The early settlers were mostly involved in agriculture and many were fiercely independent. They could afford to be so, since farming their own land and raising their own livestock, or hunting for whatever game they required made them self-sufficient. However, as the nation grew and the industrial revolution overtook it, America became an industrialized nation. Jobs in industry were plentiful and paid much more than farming with all of its uncertainty with the elements. As time progressed, increasingly more people were working in the factories than on the farms. This exposed a large number of this nation's workers to the mercy of the captains of industry and the national economy. The result was that much of the working public was losing their economic independence. Those who now controlled the economic lives of the individual became as tyrannical and ruthless as the despots they once despised. America underwent the agony of sweatshops, child labor, profit before compassion and long hours of work for short pay. Since the good will of man could not be counted on to remedy this situation, the federal government was mandated to institute laws to protect the workers. Consequently, there was enacted the anti-trust laws, the child labor laws, workman's compensation laws, workman's fair practice laws and the right to form labor unions.

Now the masses yearned for economic freedom. Oh! If only they could force the captains of industry to be fair with them. A fair share of the profits and enough time off to enjoy it, was all that the workers wanted. Therefore, armed with the right to form unions and finally the right to strike, the labor movement set out on its crusade to free the workers of this nation from economic bondage. The Great Depression sidetracked their movement for awhile, but recovery did come and people went back to work. However, the economic climate was not yet right for the big push. Then came World War II. This was the opportunity that the labor unions were waiting for! The entire American industry was working full force for the war effort. The union movement struck! America was to view the sorry spectacle of civilian workers refusing to produce the essential implements of war, or provide the raw materials required to make them. Labor went on strike until they got more pay and better benefits, while their sons died fighting in many foreign lands. The steel workers, the coal miners and workers in other essential industries, using war time as leverage, forced management to conceded to their demands and won unheard of concessions from them. By the time the war ended, the labor unions found themselves in a strong position in the labor market and with their war chests bulging with dues paid by the rank and file.

Although World War II ruined the world economy, it made the United States of America only stronger and more prosperous. This only encouraged the labor movement to be more adventurous with its demands. What started out as a justifiable movement to stop the abuses of management against labor, turned into a tyranny worse than the condition it was to remedy. As the world economy recovered, with American help via the Marshall Plan, this movement became active in England and Europe as well as in the United States.

Again the common man exhibited a tyranny equal to any of the oppressors scorned by their forefathers. The labor unions became unreasonable! They struck not for justifiable issues, but for pay far exceeding their worth and for luxuries. The use of the strike was not for negotiations, but for economic blackmail. They took "a public be damned," attitude and purposely chose those times to go on strike that was most inopportune for the public. In the 1950s, 60s and early 70s, the nation was put through agonies of labor strikes. A great number were against private and public transportation facilities that left its citizens stranded in airports, train and bus stations and sometimes unable to get to work. Frequently they struck public transportation just before Christmas time and during other essential public events. Most often the public welfare was totally ignored. The labor leaders, encouraged by their rank and file, became as unreasonable and as dictatorial as any mighty medieval potentate. Not only did they call strikes for trivial purposes, but some even resorted to anarchy. Workers frequently used violence against the property of their employers, as well as those who did not agree with them or attempted to cross their picket lines. Some unions even made alliances with the underworld and became infiltrated with racketeers. Other labor unions became fronts for organized crime and were used to launder money or move stolen or contraband merchandise. The large sums of money, which were made available to some unions in the form of pension funds, were sometimes misused or appropriated illegally. Racketeering in labor unions became so prevalent by the 1960s, that the federal government prosecuted many who were involved and passed and enforced laws to curb this abuse.

Who would have believed that a proud people, who dreamed and fought for liberty and the end of tyranny, could in just a few generations become so tyrannical and oppressive themselves. In England, the labor force became a political party that turned their once vital prosperous industries into rusty decay. The French were to also suffer as a result of the labor movement. France became so unionized, that the unions could paralyze the entire nation in just a short while by calling for a general strike.

The United States Government recognizing the potential for union chaos in this country and responding to the pressure put on them by the public and the industrial lobbies, passed remedial labor laws curtailing the powers of the labor unions. The resulting legislation did not please everyone. The union representatives believed that this legislation went too far and management and conservative thinking people felt that these laws did not go far enough. Although anti-labor laws curbed some of their abuses, it did not prevent the labor unions from disrupting the national economy. They initiated a wage and inflationary spiral which plagued the American economy for decades. The unions refused to acquiesce to any moderation or restraint. Labor's appetite for more and more pay and bigger and better benefits, became insatiable. They fought for years for a 40 hour week. Once they obtained it, they agitated for overtime and then double overtime on weekends; by the 1970s they were clamoring for a 30 hour week!

The American union workers became the spoiled brats of the labor market. They cared not that their increases in wages and benefits only caused increase in prices. They did not care that as they prospered, like no other workers since the beginning of time, that the inflation they were helping to create was causing hardships to those on fixed incomes and the poor. Like any despot, they reveled in their new found wealth and free time, and cared naught for the ills they caused others. The freedom to form unions and to strike were rights, like so many of our others, which were perverted by the common man. They turned a legitimate need into an unrestrained instrument that exceeded the bounds of reason.

The nation was ultimately presented with the perverse situation of garbage collectors being called sanitation engineers, janitors being called maintenance engineers and both receiving higher salaries than schoolteachers and other college graduates. Even as the advancement in industrial technology eliminated the need for certain jobs and could make their products and services cheaper, the unions countered with the ridiculous practice of featherbedding. This perversion of a basic American right was so blatant, that it dislocated the structure of wage parity for the entire nation. This perversion had led to an inequality between a workers occupation and its justifiable remuneration.

These practices resulted in an inequitable situation in the American work force. Those who trained and studied to perfect certain skills, were not rewarded for their efforts at the same rate as those who had spent little or no time acquiring basic repetitive skills. Therefore, in order to adequately reward those with acquired skills to reflect their true worth, salaries had to be raised to the extent that they caused the cost of the products or services performed to reflect this outrageous increase. This in turn, led to more inflation and the higher cost of everything.

The plea to organized labor by the economic community that their practices would someday price them out of the labor market, fell on deaf ears. In their arrogance, the labor unions and those they represented felt sure that they were so essential that they could blackmail the American industries forever. Their affluence blinded them to the resurgence of the economies of Europe and the Far East. As American labor became secure in their perverse labor practices, their complacency undermined the quality and efficiency of the national production. Across the seas, however, the foreign labor forces hungry for American markets increased its standards of quality and production efficiency. The challenges which had been discarded by this nation's labor force was picked up by those of West Germany, Japan and others. These nations using the dedication that American labor and industry had lost, went on to surpass the quality and efficiency of American production; the hallmark of our nation.

By the 1970s and 80s, many American union workers found themselves as oppressed by labor as they were previously by management. Their own unions had turned into bureaucratic organizations with executive officers that were paid as well as some of the presidents of the board of directors in industry. In many unions there was despotism, favoritism, nepotism, prejudice and disregard for the rights of the workers. Union officials and shop stewards were picked for their loyalty to the officers of the union, rather than for their concern for their union brothers.

In some unions, to the detriment of the rank and file, sweetheart contracts were negotiated by labor and management. As disillusionment with the labor movement spread, large numbers of its members abandoned their unions. Some members, in order to preserve their unions, attempted to use the democratic process to vote the old guard out; only to be met with anarchy and violence. These actions led to the murder of a number of union crusaders and labor executives.

Suddenly, by the latter part of the 1970s and the beginning of the 1980s, the unbelievable happened! The prophecy of the American economic community came true. Foreign labor was gradually replacing American labor and the American workers had in many industries truthfully priced themselves out of the labor market. Foreign products had become cheaper and of better quality than those made in this nation. Now the words, "made in Japan," imprinted on the back of items, no longer represented junk made from American scrap metal to be ridiculed. Instead they were now products of quality and durability. American companies could now ship raw materials or parts to foreign countries, where their labor could make the product. Once completed, the finished product could be transported back to this country and sold at a cheaper price than those produced by American labor. Now there was a ready and skilled labor markets in a number of foreign countries, that were willing to manufacture or assemble for American industry. This labor worked long hours for less pay, were more dedicated in their work ethics, and did not go on strike. As a consequence of the lost of American markets both abroad and in our country and the availability of other less expensive overseas labor markets, the United States Labor movement lost its strangle hold on this nations industries.

The party was over for the labor unions in America. They had perverted the basic concept of true unionism by disregarding the principal of honest negotiations attempted in good faith. This plus their tyrannical abuse of their economic power had caused their demise. Union membership is now the lowest in years. Many of the benefits, they frequently earned by economic blackmail, are being lost. The most unfortunate results of all, however, is that they were instrumental in the loss of many of America's largest industrial markets to foreign competition, which resulted in the closure of vast numbers of American factories that put many thousands of people out of work. Where are those high paying jobs for little skills now? Many of these one time high paid production workers, who had no transferable skills and were too old to retrain, are still out of work or doing menial jobs. This time for pay befitting their skills.

The American democratic system is based on the golden rule, that expects its citizens to arbitrate in good faith with concern for the welfare of others as well as themselves. As long as these basics were adhered to by the labor movement, ours was a powerful, prosperous industrial nation. Once those who managed industry and later those who organized labor became tyrannical and perverted these basics, the rewards of democracy deceased and with it some of their security and prosperity.

While we were busy cheating and taking advantage of one another, those less fortunate of the world found it easy to lure our prosperity away from us. The final outcome is still in question. Every year bigger and cheaper foreign labor markets are appearing. Recently, we note the emergence of the twin factory system between the industries of the United States and those of Mexico. American industries have built factories close to the American-border in Mexico. Now parts, that are made in this country, can be transported south of the border to be assemble into the finished product in these factories by cheap Mexican labor. With the vast, cheap, and eager labor market in that under-privileged country, this presents an even bigger threat to American labor. Unless Americans, both in labor and management, forget the grievances of the past and return to basic American principles, they will not only do grave injury to each other, but to the future of the United States of America as a strong industrial nation.

Our post World War II experiences should have taught us a lesson. When we teach our skills and technology to other peoples of the world, and keep their factories busy so that their work forces acquire rapid skills and efficiencies, we in reality are creating our own competition. We are giving away, for the sake of cheap labor, experiences and technical advances to other nations which has taken us decades to acquire. In addition many of these nations do not have our sense of justice and stability. This creates a climate where they could find it to their advantage to nationalize American factories and then locate their own markets for their products. Thus resulting in acquiring not only the market, but also the facilities at our expense.

For American industry to attempt to punish American labor in this manner, for its sins of the past, is like spitting at the sky. Instead of looking for more ways to pervert the American economic system, management and labor should try to find a way which not only benefits then individually, but the nation as a whole. The fruits of American's ingenuity should belong to the American people, not to those who acquire it by default. Recently, new preferential tariff agreements may further encourage American industry to seek cheap labor markets in other parts of the world.

Now that management has the upper hand, will it like the despots of the old turned into tyrants? Then will this be followed again some day by the rise of labor and more perversion? Or will management's present effort to circumvent the needs of labor in its own nation, be the final perversion that will not only prevent any future revival of labor strength, but result in the total demise of the United States as an industrial nation? Perhaps this time, the loss of American prosperity may be just around the corner!

Another American liberty had been perverted. The right for free men to form unions and strike in order to protect themselves from the abuses of management is a fundamental right of all working people. It is only when this basic right is implemented without restraint and without the welfare of the nation in mind, that it becomes perverse. Labor must realize that it is an integral part of this nation's economy, and that its goals cannot stand alone. To ask for what is reasonable is responsible. To demand without regard or restraint is perverse.

CHAPTER II

When the United States of America was still young, children were raised and educated by methods that the experiences of the past had proven to be the best. These practices were based on philosophies that had been developed over the ages and further refined by religious and social traditions of each culture. These proven methods had for generations produced adults and students with sufficient discipline and education to allow them to go on to become good citizens, parents, spouses and skilled craftsmen and professional people. This mode of raising and teaching children had resulted in the development of some of the finest and most exemplary people in the history of man and womankind.

With the dawn of the scientific age, all that was practiced in the past was held up by the scientists against the theories of their new sciences. This was done to see if the old methods measured up to the criteria conceived by these new prophets. In the same manner in which the fields of medicine, chemistry, physics, psychiatry and others were examined, so similar scrutiny were applied to the raising and education of children. These gurus of the modern methods of investigation, after using their new scientific methods which employed the use of laboratory role models composed of mice, monkeys and two way mirrors, decided that the old method of raising and educating children was incorrect. Unfortunately, these learned men did not believe in the old adage that, "the proof of the pudding is in the eating." They were convinced that there had to be something wrong with anything that did not measure up to their criteria, It did not make any difference to them if older methods, that had passed the test of time, produced good results or not. If they did not conform to these scientific postulates, they were considered incorrect and in need of restructuring.

The opinions of these investigators where at first scoffed at by a public, who where satisfied with the results of their traditional methods and saw no advantage in changing them. For years these so called, "educators," and child psychologists clamored to test their theories in the school systems and on the newborn, with little success.

However, as newer generations entered the child rearing years, the mental attitude of the public had changed. This generation was convinced, by the equally new methods of mass communication, that everything in print was truth and that these truths were found in books that gave proper instruction to the performance of all tasks. The mothers of the past took their instruction from their own mothers and grandmothers, who had a wealth of experience rearing their own children in the large families of that era. By the end of the 1940s and into the 1950s, this new generation of women were convinced that whatever they did should be, "modern." Therefore, ignoring any advice given to them by their mothers and grandmothers, these mothers sought books which they felt would instruct them in the proper way of raising children. This era coincided with the new fad of taking the newborn to a pediatrician instead of the family doctor, a measure encouraged by the obstetricians who were promoting the specialty approach to the practice of medicine.

These new physicians, unlike the older general practitioners, encouraged mothers to embrace the advice in books by medical professional on the new theory of rearing children. These books were based on one major premise, which unfortunately happened to be flawed. This premise was: that within every newborn individual lay some wonderful potential intelligence, inclinations and personalities, which if allowed to develop without restrictions and suppressions, would blossom out into the formation of an individual of highly desirable personality and abilities. Permissiveness was the cornerstone of this modern philosophy; which taught that children should not be disciplined, corrected, or overly regimented, so that they could express themselves freely at all times.

This method of child raising was enthusiastically adopted and practiced by a large number of parents of the 1940s and 50s. These new methods were readily adopted by those in the young, well educated, and affluent group, as well as those with little ties to the Old World. Some ethnic groups, however, who still venerated the advice of the elderly, paid little attention to these new methods that were being proposed. The number of parents that did follow these new methods, however, was large enough to change the character and outlook of American society for a number of generations to come.

Two other factors appeared at this time, coinciding with this new method of child rearing, to further change the character of the new American society. One was: the sudden economic prosperity that occurred in this nation, which ushered in low unemployment and wages and benefits at an all time high. Many of these new parents had been raised during a depression and they had known mostly frugality and want in their childhoods. Now with their new found prosperity, they desired to give their children everything they themselves had been denied.

The second factor: which was an event that took this nation quite by surprise, was the launching of the world's first satellite, "sputnik," by the Russians. America was shocked that another nation was able to beat them to a technical breakthrough in one of the fields of science. America's over inflated ego was punctured. Suddenly, this nation went into an academic hysteria. Everyone was blaming everyone else! What was wrong with our engineers? What was wrong with our academic institutions? How could a technically backward nation like the USSR beat us to one of the most startling technical achievements of mankind? Someone or something had to be blamed!

This was the opportunity for which the new educators were waiting! Like termites, they crawled out everywhere from under the woodwork. They were sure they had the answers to all these problems. Had they not claimed for years that America had an archaic method of teaching the young? Children were too regimented, subjects too rigid and discipline too harsh. Children were bored, the atmosphere was too grim, they weren't having any fun. What was needed was new mind expanding subjects, a less rigid manner of teaching and less restrictions. Everything must be thought differently! We needed new math, new phonetic methods of spelling, the teaching of more creative and imaginative writing and the reading of more contemporary, pertinent books.

The public eager to redeem their country's lost academic reputation for being first in everything, were easily convinced by their outcry that a change was needed. Therefore, this nation in a few short years discarded an educational system which had produced some of the greatest minds in history, for an unproven, radical and ultra liberal system of education. We had thrown the baby out with the bath water! As a result of these new methods of raising children, American parents became children worshipers. In the old philosophy children were encouraged to be seen but not heard. In this new one, the opposite was true. When children spoke parents listened. Now in the family unit, when children had something to do or say, adults stopped what they were doing or saying and turned their attention to the children. In company, interruptions were tolerated and not discouraged. Children were encouraged to voice their opinions, and to disagree when their opinions were contrary to those of their parents or other authority figures. No material necessities were denied these new privileged offsprings. If Dad did not have the money, he borrowed it or bought what the child required on credit. Under this new concept of raising children, the rod was not only spared; it was abolished. Children were to be reasoned with, not struck. Any reprimand had to be explained to them, not dictated. The family unit was now an open forum, and every member of the family had a voice in it. In addition, parents were not to be authoritarian figures; they were to be pals and friends to their children. Most important of all, children were not to be repressed, it was strongly urged that they be able to express themselves freely at all times.

In the school as well as in the home, new methods were employed. Teachers were to change the manner in which they would teach all these unrepressed and expressive children. The classes would be broken into groups according to the students accomplishments, so that the gifted child would not suffer by being inhibited by the less endowed. Teachers would have to become the children's friends.

It was also strongly urged, that discipline not be so overly harsh as to suppress the students initiative. Then there was the new math, the new method of teaching spelling, the new way of writing and the new books to read. All those old stuffy books had to go! The classics were boring. Children had to be stimulated. Consequently, the required reading was now from a list of contemporary books, which were thought to be more pertinent to the student's interests. It was also decided that children needed more than just basic education. They were in dire need of arts, crafts, hobbies and interest clubs. In addition, what would a sound mind be without a sound body? Therefore, the new educators urged more physical education for the students. Plain old exercising was considered to be too boring for these strongly motivated children. For this reason, it was decided that every child should be taught to perform one sport well.

Suddenly in the 1960s and 1970s, schools were rebuilt, remodeled or expanded to include swimming pools, tennis courts, hockey fields, soccer fields or any other sports for which the school boards could acquire money. The schools in addition obtained music rooms filled with instruments, hobby rooms filled with all necessary supplies and auditoriums the size of theaters complete with scenery, lighting and public address systems. The cost of all this resulted in a skyrocketing of the school taxes for the residents of the community. However, the public was convinced that all these acquisitions were necessary in order to keep their nation ahead in the new technical world. In addition, this country at that time was in the mist of great prosperity, and so the public dug deeper into their pockets and came up with the additional revenue to built these new monuments devoted to the reverence of children.

Now that the sciences had created a new type of child, they found it fitting that they also be given a new social position in society. This new status was that of, "the teenager," or as the more scientifically oriented preferred to refer to them, the adolescent. Then this term had to be further qualified as the pre-adolescent or the post-adolescent stage of development. Now there was no longer just adults and children. There were instead young children, teenagers, young adults, middle age adults, elderly adults and old age adults. In this manner there came into existence, "the teenager."

The new media of television, Madison Avenue and Hollywood were quick to see the possibilities offered by this fast growing number of newly classified children. The post war baby boom promised to produce an extremely large supply of them. Therefore, these opportunists wasted no time in indoctrinating this new class of children into how they should dress, act and what they should buy. The purchasing power of this group was projected to be in the billions, and their impact was soon to be felt by the type of music, wearing apparel, entertainment and cosmetics, demanded by these young Americans. These image producing elements portrayed the teenagers as rebellious, self-centered children who were incessantly on the telephone and addicted to outrageous music, attire, hairstyles and methods of entertaining themselves. With these impressions as their role model, the American teenager wasted little time in their attempt to mimic these images.

Once more a right had been perverted. The rights of children were liberalized to the extent that exceeded all bounds of reasonableness. The common man had adopted as their guide the world of science, which had convinced them that they had found, with their infallible modern scientific methods, the true answers to all problems. In doing so, they had helped create generations of children that would grow up to be adults that would make much mischief in America, and were poorly equipped to cope with the realities of the world.

The scientific community, with their new found arrogance, now began to meddle in the affairs of the family. In their eagerness to demonstrate the infallibility of their investigative methods, they tempered their findings not by good common sense, but by blind faith in the conclusions that they had attained. The results of statistics took the place of reason and contemplation and wisdom was replaced by numbers and conjecture. In the manner of the inquisitors of old, they pressed their unyielding convictions on a public easily duped by their awe in anything complicated and labeled scientific. Like the false prophets predicted in the Bible, these new men and women of science went about making chaos out of order and perverting the basic values of American society.

They had succeeded in producing a society where spoiled children, the product of an over permissive system that was totally without discipline and educated in a self-centered environment, were given the rights of adulthood. These undisciplined children without any experience or worldly knowledge now pretended to dispute the wisdom of the adults, and conclude that those who were not young were wrong about everything. The mass media were quick to invent catch phrases to characterize the phenomena they were observing.

Suddenly the American people found that there was a generation gap, a credibility gap, an age gap; people over 30 were not to be trusted by the young; the previous generations had caused all the misery in the world and the establishment was hypocritical and not to be trusted. All at once, these children without knowledge or insight were told by society that they had the same right to voice and have their opinions considered as did the adults. They were encouraged to make their thoughts and conclusions known to the members of the establishment. Showing a greater tyranny than even their elders, they set about to enforce their childish views of the world upon a tolerant nation.

 ˙ The rebellion of the American children occurred at the same time as the civil rights movement was in progress. The minorities in this nation, finding themselves excluded from the democratic process, used public demonstrations to attract the attention of their government and the people. The rebellious children did not chose to wait until they were adults to use their electoral rights. Therefore, they adopted the methods of the civil rights movement to bring their views to public attention. However, being undisciplined children, their immaturity resulted in their producing what amounted to a national tantrum. Encouraged by their doting parents, a manipulative press and their own arrogance, they resorted to anarchy and sedition to force their opinions on a mature, knowledgeable and experienced government and public.

 By the use of mob rule they disrupted our academic institutions and our free and open forums. They in addition, interfered with the freedom of speech by our political leaders, and condemned the decisions made by our elected representatives when they did not conform with what they thought was right. In a display never before seen in American Democratic Society, these products of over permissiveness turned their lack of discipline on all symbols of authority. They even turned upon their parents, who were supporting their ability to have the time and financial freedom to engage in their usurping of the public prerogative. These spoiled children criticized their own progenitors for their materialism and affluence which made their creation possible.

The non-adults of America had organized themselves, with the help of the ultra liberal and other subversive factors, into a perverted tyrannical mob. Finally the world found out what was deep inside every individual crying out to express itself! It was not amiability, beauty and light, but unbridled arrogance, conceit, lack of understanding and tyranny. Too late it was discovered that lack of discipline and the rearing of children without proper values did not develop mature, reasonable human beings, but unthinking, uncaring, disheveled, hostile and unreasonable children who were bent on destroying anything that represented authority. These children pretending to be adults had no respect for law, police, academic institutions or the decisions made by a government of adults that did not represent their childish immature views. In truth, tyranny did not lay only in the soul of the common man, but also in the marrow of their children. As their parents had perverted the rights of its society, so had its children perverted those rights which should have never been given to them in the first place.

This change in the rearing of children did not only cause disruption in the academic and political institutions, with their demonstrations, sit-ins, civil disobedience, draft evasion and other illegal acts, but it also affected the harmony in the home. Previous to this era of permissiveness, the majority of children were influenced mostly by their parents, teachers and clergy. These authority figures, more or less, guided the young and regulated the types of influences to which these impressionable youths were exposed. The young were considered minors and under the supervision of their parents until they had reached the age of maturity, which was the age of 21. It was believed that women matured faster than men at the age of 18, although, in most legal matters the age of 21 was considered the age at which both sexes became adults. The majority of minors lived with their parents until they reached the age of maturity.

With the advent of the modern age and the changing mode of raising and educating children, these old traditional views were being challenged by the young in many homes. At the same time, with the invention of television and the development of an affluent mobile society, in which many minors had their own automobiles, the influence of the parents and other authority figures began to wane.

Children who came from homes where traditional values still flourished, came under tremendous pressure from their friends and schoolmates as well as from the standards held up to them by the drive-in movies and television. The parents and other sources of supervision did not have any control over these outside influences. This resulted in the common use of another new term, parroted by the new prophets of behavior in the field of psychology," peer pressure," This psychological expression became the ultimate excuse for all that these misguided youths perpetrated.

As a consequence of these changes, in many homes where the new manner of child rearing was not practiced, conflict developed between the parents and their children. These outside influences from friends, classmates, motion pictures, television and Madison Avenue, caused many children to rebel against the traditional values of their parents. Fathers were horrified when their sons appeared with long hair, beads and strange attire. Mothers were equally disturbed when their daughters appeared at home with disheveled hair, wrinkled dresses, without bras, bands around their heads and beads and leather straps around their necks and wrists. They talked different, acted different and showed nothing but disdain for those who had their best interest at heart. They no longer considered themselves as minors. They were, "teenagers," a status which they believed gave them special privileges and entitled them to perform special rites denied other age groups.

This resulted not only in disharmony in many families, but also in heartbreak and tragedy. The guidance of their children was no longer in the hands of mature reasonable adults, but instead entrusted to the whims of immaturity and to those who would take advantage of the young and unsophisticated. Many of the permissive parents condoned the unsupervised actions of their children. Others struggled to maintain their supervision, but in the end lost total control over their children's behavior. Still others had the strength and faith to hang onto their authority at all costs.

Then there were those parents, that both worked and had no time to supervise their children, they lost control over them by default. The appearance of large numbers of minors, totally undisciplined and unsupervised by adults, led to a crisis in American society. The number of juvenile delinquents greatly increased, large numbers of children ran away from home, teenage prostitution increased and death due to drunken driving by the young became an American disgrace. Sex became a national obsession with the young, resulting in a large number of unwed mothers and causing the number of cases of venereal disease to increase in this age group. Finally there was the meanest cut of all! Drugs became a part of the adolescent's scene.

The older generation looked on in dismay! They always believed prosperity and freedom would produce an even more beautiful and righteous America. They thought that the promise of many more bountiful years to come, would produce generations of healthy, wonderful, well mannered, respectful and brilliant children. Instead, they viewed in horror a generation of children who were bent on destroying themselves and all the institutions that would restrain them. They awoke one morning to ask, "Where has all the beauty gone? What happened to all the beautiful music and the well mannered and refined children? Where has all the stylish attire, worn in good taste, gone? What happened to all those, respectful, courteous, intelligent and rational children? Who had stolen our children's innocence?" Those who created this chaos did not respond. In their arrogance they would not acknowledge their mistakes. They only invented more psychological explanations for these phenomena and then blamed society for their cause.

Chapter III

During World War II, because of the war effort, women were first accepted into jobs ordinarily held by men. It was soon discovered that many women were suitably to do tasks that once were considered not to be adaptable to the female personality, body build or strength. Difficulties that were anticipated to occur between the sexes at the job site did not materialize and with time and their constant presence, women were accepted as fellow employees. When the war ended American industry changed from the manufacture of war material to the production of civilian consumer's goods. There was a tremendously large market waiting for these new products which were in small supply during the war. As soon as industry had retooled for production of these civilian goods, there again came the need for an expansion of the labor force. This time many women had acquired those skills which were transferable to the production of these postwar products.

Women, therefore, now found many jobs for which they were suitable, that were not available to them before the war. In addition, many wives and mothers had became accustomed to working and taking care of their homes and children, while their spouses were fighting the war. When their husbands returned, many women stopped working for awhile, but they missed the extra money and independence. This resulted in a certain amount of conflict between working wives and their newly returned husbands. However, the years in the Armed Services had made many men more liberal in their views towards their wives. Also, the post war inflation and increases in salaries made it attractive for two persons to be working in the same family. Therefore, many women returned to work, or continued working, believing that they would only do so until they again reached some financial stability. However, after a few recessions and run away inflation, many married couples were not willing to change their life styles by limiting their income by only the male working. In many families, what started out as a temporary arrangement turned into a permanent one.

The freeing of women from what had always been their traditional roles, gave many of them a new feeling of independence. This led some of them to believe that they no longer should be subservient to the male, and ushered in a new wave of feminist sentiments. At the same time, many husbands themselves felt a certain amount of freedom for not being responsible for the total support of the household. They were willing to lose some of their male dominance in return for a working partner to share their expenses. These events set the stage for a turnabout which raised havoc with the family unit and the role of women in the family, as well as in society as a whole. Another right was about to be perverted; women's rights. Since the founding of this great democracy, women were viewed as a formidable force in the family unit. They had the venerated role of mother and wife. So highly regarded was the woman's role in her function as the family matriarch, that these sentiments were expressed in such quotations as, "The hand that rocks the cradle." "rules the world," or, " Father works from sun to sun, but mother's work is never done." to honor her.

However, from the time that a free society was established in America, there developed a small group of women who objected to women being excluded from constitutional protection. In the early 1900s, they organized into political organizations which ultimately resulted in the formation of, The National Women's Suffrage Association, that culminated in the acquiring of female suffrage (the right to vote) in the 1920s. The women's rights organizations in America were frustrated by Supreme Court decisions following this victory, until the civil rights upheaval arose during this century.

The advent of the civil rights movement in America led to the passage of civil rights legislation. This redefinition of civil liberties opened up avenues for other fractions that believed their rights were being infringed upon and encouraged them to come to the forefront. These events encouraged those women with feminist inclinations, that had recently won some measure of independence from traditional female responsibilities, to press for even greater release from their female role. The feminist movement was originally composed of a number of splinter groups, some conservative with legitimate complaints, others very liberal and militant and some bordering on the lunatic fringe.

In the 1970s, along with the civil rights movement, came the sexual revolution in America. This in turn, fostered freedom of sexual expression which led to the unmasking of a large population of male and female homosexuals in this nation. A number of female homosexuals, with their characteristic aversion to the male, and other women with real and imagined hostility towards the opposite sex, banded together to form the most militant and vocal of the women's rights organizations. Unfortunately, in the news media, as it is true in other circles, "the squeaky wheel gets the most grease." Therefore, the news media concentrated mostly on the coverage of this small militant group, giving the appearance that they spoke for the majority of women in the rights movement. In this way, the most radical of all groups gained a major platform to expound its doctrines.

Unfortunately, sexual animosity became confused with the major issues, and what started out as a women's rights organization turned into a movement to totally masculinize women. With the encouragement of television, who saw in the opinions of this group a controversial subject to sensationalize in its news and talk shows, the gospel as expounded by these devotees to the total domination of America by the female was daily trumpeted to the home bound housewives by daytime television. These views influenced some women to feel that they were being subjugated by their husbands and children and that they needed to emancipate themselves. Many women, already having been convinced by daytime soap operas into believing that their lives were dull, were easily lulled into dissatisfaction with their lot. From these subtle implications came the assumption that to be only a housewife was demeaning. Many women suddenly began to feel that to be only a mother and subservient to a male as sole support of the household, was beneath their dignity. These sentiments helped the feminist movement to gain some support among a section of the female population.

This further encouraged this most militant of women's movement to be even more radical in their demands. They purported that women should be equal to men in all things. Their platform was not limited to the attaining of equality for women in the work place, daycare centers for women workers, maternity pay, freedom from male sex harassment and other rights that were legitimate aspirations for women workers to seek. No! They wanted much, much, more. What they seeked was the perversion of the liberties of the female gender.

It seems that tyranny does not only lie within the fibers of men and children, but also in the inner corners of the female soul. Like the tyrants of old, from which their forebears had fought so desperately to free themselves, these women set upon a course that would totally disrupt the foundation of the democratic society in which they lived. They cared not if it was right for their children, husbands, or society at large, as long as they felt it was right for them. "Do your own thing baby," became the slogan for these women, some who would abandon their husbands and children.

To pervert our basic rights, one has only to accentuate the positive. If one follows this line of reasoning, then if suppression of a person's rights is evil, then to extend them should be good. Therefore, in the minds of these misguided women, the more an individual's liberties are increased the better should be the final results. However, the truth is that perversion is the absence of all restraint. Any liberty without restrain; is perversion. Women, as in the case of other groups such as, gender, age, race, or ethnic groups, have rights. However, these rights should not be extended to the degree that the absence of any perimeters, whatsoever, leads to utter chaos. If women are to have rights without restrictions, then they will have been given the privilege of denying their responsibilities and commitments to anyone and anything.

A family unit cannot exists without the maternal allegiance of the female partner. If one has no regard for civilized behavior, regardless of whether it be based on religion or tradition, then one had better pay attention to the laws of nature. It is often incomprehensible, that those who may be so intent on not disturbing the ecology about them, will have little qualms in destroying the equilibrium of the most important of all natural phenomena; the family. In the scheme of nature, whether one believes in a divine being or natural selection, mankind, or indeed any breed of animal, cannot exist without the natural duties of each gender. If it were not for the fierce protection of its mother, few grizzly bears would survive the violence of the male partner. When lionesses have cubs, their ferocity exceeds even that of the mighty male lion. These examples, as simple and unsophisticated as they appear, seem to elude those women who would change the natural balance of nature to satisfy a desire to fit an image created by confused, bitter, self-centered and unfeminine women. A woman is nature's or God's finest creation. To conceive, create, bear and rear a child is truly one of this world's great miracles. This fact can best be appreciated by those women who cannot bear one. In the natural order of things, a family is composed of a mother, father and children. In this order each is equipped, by whatever creator there be, to perform certain functions.

The male is bigger and stronger not to overpower the female, but to protect her. The female is smaller and more gentle, not so that she may be dominated by the male, but so that she can give a measure of much needed emotional balance to the family structure. Males being stronger and more hostile, have the ability to roam unprotected not because they are superior to the female, but because they are equipped by nature to protect themselves. By their physical structure and temperament, each sex is endowed with those characteristics that make it possible for a man and woman to live together and bear offspring to perpetuate the race.

These basic factors feminists prefer to ignore. Their philosophy is based on envy for the traits and the life style of the male. Such women do not want rights; they want to be males. They, in their misguided view, resent the fact that women are not endowed with those attributes and do not live the type of life style that they find appealing in the male. The feminist believes that what a male does and the type of life he leads is superior to theirs, and they wish to imitate them. The only way that they can achieve this goal, is to destroy the natural, traditional role of the female and substitute those of the male. In attempting to do this, they are upsetting the balance of nature. When one attempts to alter this balance, inevitably nature has a way of striking back!

A family with a truant mother is a very weak unit. Men can perform the duties of mothers, but they are poor imitations. There is no substitute for the natural mother in rearing children. There is no substitute for a mother in producing an atmosphere of comfort and security in the home. There is no substitute for the efforts of a mother in protecting the health and welfare of her children. Finally, there is no more important, natural, maternal duty for a women than to be a mother. It will take several generations of motherless women, who have chosen a masculine life over what they were intended by nature to be, before their shallow existence, loneliness and sorrow will convince other women that this is not the way.

The feminist movement far from liberating women has made them slaves to their own new life styles. There are few women who have become editors, fashion designers, grand entrepreneurs or captains of industry. Most women far from being liberated and finding new enriched lives and interesting occupations, have in truth only been burdened with added responsibilities. In addition, they have lost the traditional protection of the male leaving themselves exposed to a hostile and violent society. The average, so called liberated woman of today, is not fulfilling some life-long desire to perform some lofty ambition repressed within her soul. Instead, she is the overburdened wife and mother who must arise at six o'clock in the morning so that she can get her children off to school and take the smaller child to a baby sitter or day care center, before departing for work. She sees her children go off to school and then hands her small child to a strange woman or to a group in a daycare center. This mother then leaves for work with sadness in her heart and guilt in her soul for abandoning her responsibilities to others who have no real motherly interest in her child and the knowledge that when her children return from school they will find a lonely empty house.

Guilt ridden and tired, she must then fight her way through morning rush hour traffic, by car or public transportation, to her place of employment. Most of these women do not work in some exciting, self satisfying profession or enterprise. The majority of them work in the types of occupations that are difficult, repetitive and non-stimulating. They are the waitresses who stand on their feet all day and must put up with the ever present indignities from a fickle, ill tempered public. They are the saleswomen that work in the hundreds of thousands of small shops and large department stores across this nation, that must withstand the abuse and onslaught of a never ending number of ambivalent and bad mannered customers. They are the nurses, the dental hygienists, the technicians, the medical clerks and the secretaries, that must work in a bureaucratic medical system that becomes more chaotic everyday. They are the clerk typists, the word processors, the computer operators and secretaries, that must contend with the whims and personalities of those superiors that never recognize that there is a limit to what an employee can accomplish in a day. They are the women that work at a thousand production lines in large drafty, ill smelling, deafening noise ridden industrial plants. Factories that are filled with occupational hazards, that OSHA tries to eliminate and management tries to ignore. Then there are those women that have won the dubious prize of being allowed to do work previously considered too physically taxing for women. These privileged women can now perform these duties with bodies ill fitted for their performance, and in order not to prove management right, endure the discomfort and pain they feel in silence.

At the end of the work day, when these working women can finally return to their homes, then its back to the evening traffic jams and crowded public transports. Women have now finally earned the right to endure all the trials and tribulations once reserved mainly for the male gender. There is one difference, however! The working housewife does not return to a well kept house with supper waiting to be put on the table. Oh no! She returns home to find all those responsibilities that a mother and housewife must perform, no matter what else she does. Some husbands help: this may relieve some of the burden, but it certainly does not eliminate it. Many working women are not liberated, they have only gained added responsibilities to make their lives more difficult.

Women have paid an exorbitant price for their obsession to compete with the male counterpart. They sought freedom from housework and household responsibilities; they got long hours of work outside the house, plus those inescapable duties that all mothers and wives must perform. They sought financial independence from their husbands; they became co-supporters of the family household. The money they made did not buy them independence, but instead only a hedge against increase prices and inflation. In addition, their absence from the home caused them to incur added expenses. They had to pay a babysitter or daycare center, if they had young children. Transportation, by car or public conveyance, to and from work also ate into the family budget. An added burden, was the expense of bringing lunch to work five days a week, or eating it at a restaurant or fast food service. Then there was no time for food preparation at home, so that only pre-prepared food could be purchased, which cost far greater than food that could be prepared from basic ingredients.

In addition to all there added expenses, women soon found out that their take home pay was considerably diminished by deductions from their paychecks. There was federal withholding tax, (in most states) state withholding tax, social security tax, pension fund and health insurance premiums. Instead of independence, the married working woman was entrapped into a life style, which in order for her to maintain, would demand that she must permanently participate in a two salary household.

For those women who decided not to have children after marriage to avoid all these problems, this remedy in most cases was worst than the disease. A marriage without children is an unnatural one. The results are frequently easily visible as time progresses. At the inception of their married life, both spouses enjoy their freedom from the responsibility of having and raising children. However, as they mature with age, all those material things which both worked and strove so hard to obtain, do no longer compensate for the void they feel in their lives. It must also be realized, that there are some individuals that never reach emotional maturity. These men and women do not feel this void and probably are better off without children, since they would have been poor parents in any case. However, many married couples are motivated not by their own convictions, but by the constant rhetoric of those individuals that set the whims and fads of this new generation. They do not realize that most often the idealism of youth is short lived, but the maturity that comes with age is much longer lasting.

Some women recognize the call of their maternal instincts, and are fortunate enough to have a child before their biological clocks wind down. Many other women realize their folly too late in life, and are tremendously disappointed when they find that they are no longer fertile. Then there are those married couples who disagree about the prospect of having children after many years of a childless marriage, rationalizing that they are too old or just do not want to change their financial or life styles. Those husbands and wives whose marriages are childless by choice, have more or less only a legal contract that binds them together. They try to fill the void in their lives with pets and expensive motor cars, treating both like spoiled children. In other relationships, one spouse treats the other like a child, resulting in a spoiled, pampered partner who becomes a misfit in a mature society. Too late do they discover that youth and the satisfaction of acquiring material rewards are short lived, but the emptiness and loneliness of a home without children and a future without progeny is everlasting.

From the very beginning of human awareness, the male has been the sexual aggressor and initiated the pursuit for female sexual favors. With the gradual development of what we call civilization today, these favors were gradually, but consistently, withheld by the pressured female. The male was held in abeyance until he held some promise of being the one the female favored, and had offered a permanent relationship which was sanctioned by their society. These trends varied in proportion through the ages. During some periods of human civilization, the ability of the male to provide for the female or the advantage to one or both families of the couple to gain in their union, was paramount. Throughout the romantic periods of these cultures, the romanticized version of true love was to supersede all other factors in the willingness of the female to submit to the advances of the male.

In western civilization, the period of chivalry was soon followed by the Victorian age, during which propriety and gracefulness in all matters of love and human sexual behavior was demanded by that society. In the North American hemisphere, the eastern section of the new nation was conservative and followed these customs, and the developing new western territories, more or less, made their own rules as they went along. By the early 1920s, the United States now a nation of many races and cultures, began to integrate into the formulation of a culture of its own. Before sexual customs could be firmly ingrained into its code of conduct the invention of the moving picture came into being. The combination of these two factors, which provided a mixture of cultural background and pictorial fantasy as portrayed on celluloid film to large audiences, conceived a sexual protocol which was followed from that generation into the 1950s. This approved code of sexual behavior, provided that women would only pair off with those males that she felt a strong emotional attachment to, which was called love.

The same was true of the male. However, although sexual experimentation short of actual intercourse was allowed, a woman dare not submit totally to the male until she had found one in which there was mutual love; and only after marriage and on the honeymoon night. The fact that the male would be sexually aggressive, regardless of what the cultural code demanded, was recognized by all cultures. In this country, the fact that the male had to experiment sexually in order to someday instruct the female of his choice, was also an understood part of this sexual code. This led to the double standard custom; the male being allowed to sow his wild oats, and the understanding that nice girls did not give into the advances of the male. The reasons for these practices was quite obvious to all. Since the male seeked only sexual gratification until he found the object of his heart, while he searched, many women would be seduced along the way without any assurance that giving away their sexual favors would result in a permanent affiliation. Therefore, women who hoped for a secure, respected position in their community held fast to this cultural code. This created in our society the age old struggle between men and women; the male continually trying to seduce the female, and the females using every guile and subterfuge to resist until married by the male. Most women of those generations adhered to this code of behavior, not only for the sake of propriety, but also because of fear. There was the fear of venereal diseases. Diseases with terrible complications, for which for many years there was no reliable treatment. Then there was the fear that the male would kiss and tell, ruining the woman's reputation and spoiling her chances for a good marriage. During this period, there was a high priority for the finding of virginity in an unmarried female, since the loss of chastity was considered to be indisputable evidence of a fallen woman. Finally there was the fear of pregnancy. Until the 1960s, there was no reliable way of preventing pregnancy, and the best laid plans of men and women oft times went awry. Until the end of the 1950s, society was totally unforgiving to a woman pregnant out of wedlock. Abortions were only performed in back room fashion by unskilled untrained or unscrupulous operators and quite often resulted in great morbidity or mortality to the unfortunate woman. Therefore, these fears and the rules of sexual conduct demanded by their society, kept women from deviating from the established sexual customs of that day.

Regardless of the claims of the political rhetoric of today, the most important liberation that women gained in the 20th century, was that produced by birth control. The advent of the birth control pill freed women from their uncertainty concerning the number of children they wished to conceive and space of time between pregnancies. This was true women's liberation. Now married couples could plan financially for their children, and for the size of the family that they desired. There was no more reason for any woman to be burdened by a large family, unless she wished to do so for religious or other reasons. A newly married woman could delay pregnancy until she had a chance to be financially secure. She could practice some profession, skill or craft, until she was ready for a family. Smaller families enabled women to return to the work force, and other interests, as soon as their few children were old enough to attend school or go to a daycare center. This was one of the major factors which gave women the time for contemplation to seek even greater advances for themselves.

However, there was also a negative aspect to the newly acquired ability of women to prevent pregnancy. This removed one of the biggest deterrents to promiscuous sexual behavior in the female. Urged on by the feminist's movements ultra liberal doctrine, some women decided that anything that a man did should be considered by them as fair game to imitate. Without any real insight or serious forethought, they decried the sexual double standards of the males; as if it were a noteworthy practice that women should also engage in. Their battle cry became, "down with the chauvinist male pigs" as if some wonderful form of human enjoyment was being kept away from them.

At first the practice of women being sexually active with many partners, was distasteful to most rational, mature females. However, the media of television always ready to exploit any new fad or controversial subject for better ratings, especially with sexual connotations, featured this new concept into some of its sitcom plots. At first these presentations were very subtle, and were for the sake of comedy. It was not long, unfortunately, before television took a more blatant approach, introducing the concept of cohabitation between non-married consenting adults as a common practice. The wide spread viewing of television by the

American public, has given this media the unprecedented ability to legitimize certain radical and little excepted cultural changes by making these practices seem commonplace. In this manner, suddenly on the television screens and then quickly copied by the cinema, in practically every production unmarried women were jumping into bed or living with some male stud who never seemed to keep his shirt or pajama top on. This scene became so commonplace in every household, that in spite of the complaints of more conventional and traditional people, it soon was accepted as the norm by many in the newer generations. Suddenly a woman was no longer a harlot if she slept with a male, or lived with a man in a flagrant manner out of wedlock. What only yesterday was called promiscuous sexual behavior, suddenly became the sexual revolution. Once the perimeters of propriety were breached, it was not long before all the barriers against sexual chaos fell. The American women's basic liberties had been even further perverted. The consequences of which were to cause serious harm to many women for years to come. Another basic liberty had been perverted. The liberty that women had to find and choose a male of their liking without being pressured into sexual adventures. Women themselves have perverted their own basic sexual code. This was done by extending the basic belief that if the right for a woman to freely find and be alone in the company of a male of her liking is good, that it logically follows that unrestricted cohabitation between a woman and a man is even better. The consequences of this over liberalization of sexual behavior make it quite evident that as in other basic rights, the absence of all restraints in any liberty results in the perversion of that right.

This wave of perverse sexual freedom coursing through American society, has led to serious results which could have been predicted by any student of history or sociology. The old adage, "that there is nothing new under the sun," applies adequately here. It had all been tried before; and had not worked. From the days of the Greek and Roman Empires, to the Bohemian movement in Greenwich Village in the 1920s and 1930s; it did not work! What makes these proponents of this perverse means of living believe it will work today. The sad truth is that this sexual revolution has only resulted in the production of a record number of illegitimate children, violent acts against women, suicides among young women, cases of venereal disease, estrangement between offspring and their parents and myriads of frustrated and bitter women who have been used and then discarded by their male partner.

Contrary to the impressions created by the news media, television and the motion picture industry, the majority of American women did not succumb to the rhetoric of those women who would change all the laws of God and nature. Most women do not aspire to a life with multiple sex partners and a career in some all engulfing pursuit. Most are conservative, mature women who seek to find a suitable husband and to establish a home and have children. However, the propaganda from the feminist movement and those examples constantly exploited on television and in the cinema, do increase the percentage of the female population who accept this challenge to be liberated from what previously had been their traditional role. The result is that these practices, although not universal, do become sufficiently commonplace so that they tend to influence the opinions of those who are constantly subjected to them. Although most women do not accept these new trends, enough of them do to effect significant changes in the American moral structure.

Frequently it is not the flagrant acceptance of outrageous life styles that affects society, as much as it is the peripheral fall out that sets as acceptable new trends that heretofore were considered taboo. In this way the changes that do occur seem minor in comparison to the more radical, and are more easily accepted by the public. This is the phenomena that resulted from the feminist movement. Although most women would not support the abandonment of husbands and children by women to go find themselves or live with multiple male partners, for them to consider an occupation to be more important than their family and acquiescing to the practice of unmarried women having sexual adventures and living with a man before marriage, seemed more acceptable to them by comparison. The mass communication media by removing the shock value of certain practices, and making them commonplace by putting them daily on our television screens, legitimizes drastic changes in social norms that make them more acceptable by the general public.

The change in the natural and traditional role of women in America has raised havoc with the family unit. When only men departed the home in order to provide for the family, women were always left behind to take care of and supervise the children. In addition, it was her function to provide for the comfort, nourishment and welfare of her entire family. She was spared the rigors of being the bread winner, not because she was being discriminated against or because she was not endowed with the mental capability of doing so, but because her duties were considered already sufficiently burdensome, and too important to be abridged by other responsibilities.

This absence by women from their homes today has left a void which remains unfilled. In the morning, children are rushed off to school with minimal amount of attention, so that mom can get off to work. Small children are torn from their warm beds and carried half asleep to the homes of strangers or impersonal daycare centers full of other unhappy children, so that mother can go to work. At the end of the school day, children no longer return to their homes greeted by a smiling mother and the aroma of food cooking on the stove. Now they return to an empty home with its strange silence and absence of any welcome odor. There is no one home to greet them, no one home to share the joys of that day's accomplishments, or a shoulder to lean on to dispel the frustrations of that day's disappointments. Those who coin new words call them, "Latch key children," a better word would be "mother abandoned children."

Once home, these children have no supervision and many of them wander about the neighborhood or go to the nearest hangout, to try to find solace in the company of other children who have also been asked to return to an empty home. When mom does return home, she either has the baby in her arms and it becomes her first priority, or if her children are all of school age, she is so tired physically and emotionally that she makes no pretense at becoming the cheerful ever loving mother of the family. Some mothers by prearrangement manage to prepare an evening meal. This usually consists of pre-prepared food items put together in a microwave oven or merely defrosted and served in its own package. At other times, the children are encouraged to eat at fast food services, or go to take out food services and bring the food home to eat. In many homes the evening meal is very informal. Each member of the family provides for themselves, except any very small children. This is accepted without complaint, since everyone already is conditioned to standing instructions that mom is very tired after working all day and sacrifices have to be made by the other members of the family. By the time that the parents return home from work; the baby is attended to; the family feeds itself in some fashion; and mom and dad do some of the essential chores; there is little time for the parents to listen to the emotional needs of their children or supervise them.

Children learn to squeeze their studies and the watching of television in between all these other activities and some even leave the home after supper to get away from the chaos. When all is done, the family finally retires for the night so that they may arise the next morning and start the same process all over again. Is this anyway to run a family? You bet it isn't! Even in the animal kingdom, the female will not allow her young offspring to wander to far from the pack. She knows instinctively that in allowing them to do so, will leave then vulnerable to the predators. It is not any different with the human race. From the beginning of time, children have been supervised and protected by their mothers. The male parent was too often away from the family hearth, to provide this function consistently. In the human society, there are always the predators, many disguised in sheep's clothing, who prey on the unprotected young. Unsupervised or entrusted into the hands of others, larger and larger numbers of children are molested and abused every day. We hear daily accounts of children being physically and sexually molested and abused in daycare centers, by baby sitters, and even by counselors and members of the clergy. Only parents and especially the mother, can best protect the welfare of the children. If the children are older, then they succumb to the absence of supervision. How many children have learned to experiment with drugs, or engaged in sex in their own home, because their was no one there to supervise them? How many children have gotten into difficulty with the law, by being in locations or associating with elements that proper supervision would have prevented? Go to any mall or shopping center, or local hangout, or video arcade, immediately after school hours, and you will find hundreds of children wandering about with nothing to do, because there is no one at home to go back to.

They mill, wander and look for exciting things to do. Many stray into the path of unwholesome practices and habits. Can the acquiring of any amount of material security be worth this price? It would be far better for these children to have patches on their clothing and eat stew and boiled potatoes every night for supper, and have the constant presence of the mother to comfort, supervise and protect them. Than to be abandoned most of the day, so that they can romp about in Adadias, designer jeans and with money in their pockets to buy junk food and purchase the rudiments of their acquired bad habits. Another liberty had been perverted. The right for a woman to work outside the home in any occupation that she chose, now was perverted to include the right for women to work at the expense of the welfare of her children. When liberal minded citizens supported the right of women to work and have a career, they did not do so at the expense of the American family. It was mostly intended for those women who wanted a career instead of marriage, and for widows, divorced women and unmarried women, that they felt should not be denied the right to find and keep gainful employment. The women's movement perverted this concept to their doctrine that the ability for women to work meant their independence and freedom from the domination of the male. This liberty has been perverted to the extent that the natural duties and responsibilities that women have for the family unit, are now considered by them to be subservient. The combination of over permissiveness, selfishness, affluence, and the influence of mass communication, has produced a new generation of American women who view all of their responsibilities and natural duties as enslavement by a male dominated world.

Let us explore the term, "Women's, Liberation." For someone to be liberated, it presupposes that the individual is enslaved, dominated or incarcerated. This certainly does not describe the status of women in western civilization. The women in western cultures, especially in Anglo-Saxon nations, have always enjoyed a great deal of freedom as well as reverence and respect from the male. Unlike the women in the Latin nations where the traditions of the Roman doctrine of Patria Potestas denied them many legal rights and their cultures many freedoms. Therefore, this liberation that women speak of today, is meant by them to be freedom from those responsibilities and natural duties that a woman inherits with her sex, or from the commitment she made when she took her marriage vows. The natural duties and commitments that a woman has are not a form of enslavement from which she needs to be liberated, but responsibilities that come with her status as a member of the human race. She can be freed from these only by denying or abandoning them. In abdicating these duties, women betray not only their function in the human design, but also those contributions made by generations of women who have fulfilled their responsibilities and thereby developed human civilization as wc know it today. Those who follow a different course can only alter the balance of nature. The commitment that women enter into when they elected to marry is of their own choosing, and any denial of this pledge is a betrayal of a sacred vow. Women cannot abdicate their natural position in the human society without either feminizing the male, or masculinizing themselves. Since men are comfortable in their inherited sex role, then women can only be freed from all her female responsibilities by being masculinized. Unsex is a useless term in nature, there is no neutering or unification of sex in the natural condition and hermaphrodism is an abnormal state.

The feminist resents any comparison made between women and men. They decry as prejudice against women any attempt to even suggest that, except in the physical sense, women are different than men. The indisputable fact is: that women are different from men in ever respect. They are emotionally, mentally, as well as physically different from men. Their viewpoints are different, their thought processes are different. They react differently to stress, their competitiveness is different, their degree of hostility is different. Their bone structure is different, their pelvic sizes and configurations are different, their muscular structures are different. Their emotional mechanisms are different. In short, of course, they are different! That is what makes them women! They were designed by God, or natural selection, to perform the functions of women. To be a woman is a wonderful thing! Only self-centered, envious. frustrated, bitter, dissatisfied women, with little respect for their own sex or self worth, could preach the gospel of masculinizing their gender. Women should stop to asses their own attributes, before considering that the male is worthy of imitation.

Women are marvelous beings, let us count the ways: women are more graceful then men, they are smoother, less hairy, more esthetically attractive, they are built for speed and motion, even their genitals are built internally so that they do not dangle and get in the way. Their breasts are pointed and aerodynamically designed, they have fat pads strategically located so as to protect certain bony prominences. In addition, they are more patient, less hostile, more loving, have greater intuition, make a house a home, can create a child and produce milk to nourish that child. They give pleasure in a way that no other creature on earth can, and they even smell better than men!

God or nature has created woman in this manner so that she is adequately equipped to do those duties that have been assigned to her. She was designed so that she can perform the functions of a woman; not those of a male! As a woman the female is unique, when she attempts to imitate the male, then she is only a poor imitation. Women were created, by whatever powers there be, as a partner to their male counterpart and not their adversaries. Their place in nature's grand design was for women to be the male's partner not their competitors.

The feminist movement today is attempting to pervert, by the legislative route, the natural role of women. They are claiming that every function performed by the male and denied to them, is an infringement of their civil and constitutional rights. Those who champion this opinion base their support on the premises that since the writing of the constitution, changes in our society and culture have made some of those original concepts archaic. The fact remains, that the basic unit of society; the family, is timeless. Any attempt to change women's traditional role, by legal means, only undermines its basic structure and brings chaos to our social order and disregards the welfare of other members of the family unit; the husband and children. The changes in feminine social fashions, which are fickle at best, can be argued and legislated as the whims of time mandate them, but the moral responsibilities of women for their families cannot. The maternal obligations, like its instinct, cannot be legislated out of existence. The laws of God and nature can be tampered with, but they cannot be abolished, and in the end these laws from a higher authority will return by necessity and reason in order to terminate the chaos that their disruption has engendered. Women are attempting to obtain from man's laws, the release from feminine responsibilities that they know would not be approved of by the laws of God or nature. History has shown that man and womankind cannot usurp those laws that regulate the destiny of the human race.

The over permissiveness, affluence and the cult of self-gratification bred into the American society has also engendered arrogance into many of its citizens. Some women who have been freed from their traditional roles, and now find that they can intimidate the rest of society by merely screaming prejudice or sexual harassment at all those who stand in their way, feel that this freedom now extends into their relationship with their religion. These newly liberated women, presently believe that they can also intimidate the church into conceding to their demands. In their arrogance, they are convinced that they have the right to pick only those commandments and teachings of the church that they choose. In their misguided sense of freedom, they now envision the church as a democracy with an open forum where they have a voice in the ministry of God. They, therefore, believe that since secular laws have been passed that allows them legally to break the laws of God and nature, that almighty God and whatever powers there be, must now also acquiesce to these enactments.

This new practice of religious disobedience is found not only among the lay women members of churches, but also in the female religious orders of the Catholic church. Here we find the unbelievable spectacle of nuns attempting to dictate their terms to the highest authority of their church, the Pope.

This then, is perhaps, the most iniquitous of all the other perversions of American liberties. This in essence is liberty run amuck! This is liberty without restraint! The liberal elements of the American citizenry is so intoxicated with its contemporary demand for totally unrestricted liberties, that they now demand that they should not be subjected to the will of anyone, not even their God. Can these really be the descendants of those who so revered their God, that they came to this new land to escape religious persecution? Does anyone truly believe, that the founders of our democracy intended that their offspring should someday so pervert their liberties, that they would rebel against the laws and restrictions placed upon them by almighty God! Even those tyrannical rulers of old were fearful of usurping, or even questioning, the laws and rights of the kingdom of heaven.

When the human conscience is no longer encumbered by the laws of man, and denies the laws of God, then the lack of any restraint leads to the performance of acts heretofore deemed unthinkable. The mass destruction of the young in its mother's womb, is truly one of the greatest offenses against all the laws of God and nature. If such a program was instituted by a totalitarian regime, it would be heralded as a crime against humanity and its perpetrators tried by a world court and punished. However, in America today this act is not only legal, it is championed by the women's liberation movement as a right belonging to all women. This then, is the most perverse of all of the perversions of American liberties!

Women presently believe that since they are now liberated from all the responsibilities of their sex, that they also have the right to decide whether those conceptions, which are the result of promiscuous or irresponsible sexual activity, should live or die. Not satisfied with the chaos they are causing in the most basic unit of American society, they now demand the power to determine life or death for their unborn children. They insist that abortions should not be restricted to only indicated situations, but that it be performed indiscriminately as a means of terminating conception. When women had no effective means of contraception, abortion had always been considered a crime against nature. Now that a highly efficient method of birth control is available in pill form, many women perversely and jealously guard their right to destroy those products of conceptions which are the result of unrestrained and irresponsible sexual behavior. Abortion, as any medical procedure, is justified in those conditions in which there is a medical indication, but should not be used as some sort of post hoc contraception to tidy up an unwanted or unplanned for pregnancy. The definition of contraception is the prevention of pregnancy not the destruction of the newly created individual after it has already been conceived. The question of whether a fetus should be regarded as an individual or not, is a mute point and an exercise in semantics, since no one can argue with the fact that, unless some unforeseen prenatal calamity occurs, all fetuses will develop into a newborn child. If it were not so, then there would not be such an outcry to terminate its development.

The act of abortion is to kill the potential child in uterus so as to prevent its existence. It seems inconceivable, that those same individuals that abhor euthanasia and genocide, have no such aversions when it comes to destroying a newly created human being. They see little parallel between a member of the human race being killed in a gas chamber and then cremated in a brick oven, and one that is torn asunder while incarcerated it its mother's womb. It defies all understanding to have a society that is so concerned with any mistreatment of its pet animals, even for research purposes, and yet so dispassionate when it comes to the destruction of its own young. It seems so incongruous, to have this same society adamantly against allowing the terminally ill, who suffer untold agony, to die with dignity, and yet vehemently demand the death of their unborn children for no other reason than they are unwanted. The universal availability of effective contraceptive products makes the occurrence of unwanted pregnancies unnecessary in most cases, unless irresponsible or unrestrained sexual activity has occurred. The fact that an abortion by qualified physicians is legal and readily available, encourages those individuals who do not have the maturity or inclination to employ contraceptive measures to continue ignoring their responsibilities. Surprisingly, there has been little outcry from the public sector for an explanation of why so many women need abortions when effective measures of contraception are available? Would so many women be eager to ignore their contraceptive responsibilities if indiscriminate abortions were not available? No one argues that there are not real indications for abortion, however, birth control is not one of them. It is the height of cowardice for a mother to allow her unborn child to be destroyed because the newly created individual has no voice and is hidden away from sight in her womb. To pretend that a child does not exist until it sees the light of day, and can cry, is the deceptive mental mechanism employed by these women who cannot admit to themselves the awful truth of what they are really doing.

They dare not allow their minds to form a mental picture of who they are really destroying. It is much easier for them to imagine that the fetus within them, tucked away out of sight, has no human form and is not really a child.

Can there be any greater tyranny, than the demand for the destruction of all unwanted, unborn children by the women of any society? In addition, can there be any greater perversion, than their allegation that this act is guaranteed to them by the Constitution?

Those who favor the complete revision of women's traditional role in modern American society, justify their position on the claim that women are frequently abused by men. It would be naive to believe that all men love and respect women, or that they are all mature enough to have a true partnership with their spouses. The relationship between any two human beings is complex and when there is contemplated a lifetime association, these complexities become even greater. The changes that have occurred in American society over the last 40 years, have presented an even greater challenge to the institution of marriage and the relationship between men and women. To address these domestic problems, solutions must be found that will result in adjustment to these changes in a manner in which the family, the basic unit of society, is preserved. The answer does not lie in the abdication of women from their female responsibilities nor in the masculinization of their sex. The criminal abuse of women and the abridgment of their civil rights, should and is being remedied by legislature and judicial means. Although many women are abused physically and emotionally by their husbands or male associates, this practice is certainly not so prevalent that the entire structure of human society should be changed. In the last few decades great strides have been made in identifying these abuses, and corrective measures have already been set into place or are contemplated.

One would have to be crass and unfeeling to hold that those changes in the law or customs that reversed the common law positions that encouraged the subservient position of women in the American society, were not justified and necessary. From the Constitutional Convention to the enactment of the 19th amendment, a span of 135 years, women were excluded from many of the benefits of our constitution. It was not until the 1960s and 1970s that women were legally protected against sexual discrimination. It is not these changes that have had a deleterious effect on American society; it is the perversion of these necessary corrections, by the feminist movement, which has corrupted their intention.

CHAPTER IV

Since the beginning of human civilization, the male has been the dominant member of the family unit in most cultures. In the majority of the Eastern and Middle Eastern societies, women were totally subjected to the dictates of their male members. Those nations which arose out of the fragmentation of the Roman Empire continued to follow Roman law and traditions, and held onto their male dominated societies into the modern age. Other non-Romanized cultures, as developed in such countries as Scandinavia and the British Isle, had societies in which the male, although still a dominant figure, had more of a partnership with their spouses rather than total domination.

When America was discovered and evolved into a new nation, it developed its own culture. which was a combination of the customs found in those other societies. This new culture also had at its basic unit, the family, which as in all civilized societies consisted of a mother, father and their offsprings. The duties of the parents were those which were always traditionally performed by each sex. The female took care of the home, bore the children and reared them. The male provided food, protection and shelter for the family. Women stayed at home and were preoccupied with the welfare of the family. Meanwhile, men left the family hearth to work either in the fields or at some craft or occupation, to provide the family with the necessities of life. It was the male's responsibility to support his family. He provided the raw materials that his wife turned into meals, clothing, comforts in the home and whatever other luxuries she could manage to procure from what she received. A wife's ability to manage what her husband provided, often determined whether a household would prosper or not. A male's inability to provide adequately for his family, was looked upon by society as a failure of his ability to function as a man.

In addition to supplying the basic necessities of life for his family, the male was also responsible for furnishing them with shelter. He did this by either physically building a house, or acquiring the funds for either renting or purchasing one. His inability to do so, could spell disaster for the entire family. During the time before this nation provided aid for those who could not support themselves, the inability of a man to support his family could lead to them starving and the danger of being without a roof over their heads.

A man's duty was not restricted only to providing for his family, he was also charged with protecting them. He often did this in time of war by banding together with other men to defend his country when it was in danger. Also, he had the additional responsibility of protecting those weaker members of his family, the women and children. This meant that he had to guard against those threats to his wife and daughters from other males in the community, and to be ever vigilant to keep them out of compromising situations. Unless a man fathered sons, these duties remained solely his for the remainder of his life. Only when his children were raised and they departed home, did his responsibilities diminish.

This traditional male role remained unchanged in America until after World War II. The war years demonstrated the capability of women to function adequately in this nation's labor force. This ability for women to find work outside the home without difficulty, gave them a degree of independence never held by them before. Consequently, they put pressure on their husbands to allow them to hold jobs away from the household. At first men resisted, fearing a threat to their dominant position in the home. However, as a result of economic changes many households found it financially necessary or advantageous to have both spouses working. This resulted in a large number of women joining the work force.

As this trend continued, men for the first time experienced freedom from the total responsibility they held for providing for their families. Now that their family's welfare was not entirely dependent on them, men could change their jobs more easily, and be more discriminating in the type of employment they would accept. No longer was the male totally responsible for the burdensome obligation of being the only provider for his family. Men quickly recognized the benefits that they received with the change in traditional roles between them and their wives, and were willing to give up some of their dominance in the family unit to receive them. Ultimately, with the passage of time, the male no longer considered his wife's desire to work as a voluntary choice on her part, but as a responsibility she incurred when she agreed to marriage. As a result of these changes, men were finally liberated from this weighty responsibility which in the past was theirs from the day of their marriage unto the grave.

The proud stance taken by women in their claim to be liberated, is a farce! It is the men who have been truly liberated! This liberation of men from their family obligations led to other ramifications. Men now felt less inhibited in acquiring personal luxuries and spending money exclusively for themselves, secure in the knowledge that their wife's salary would cover any deficiencies generated by them. Also, many men felt less anguish in discarding their wives for younger and more attractive women, since they were no longer burdened by the guilt of leaving their families without any means of support. In addition, because their wives had abandoned the family hearth to help provide for the family, men now felt that it was impossible for them to shield their wives from the acts and attention of other men. Therefore, they no longer felt they needed to look after the welfare of their wives in this respect, and expected that they would fend for themselves. Many men also believed that women were attempting to acquire masculine roles. Therefore, they felt justified in abandoning all male courtesies towards women, as well as any restraint of masculine crudness in their presence.

A male's biological maturity is paralleled by an ever increasing sex drive. As soon as a young man matures, he is constantly preoccupied with the seduction of willing females. This is a biological fact and has nothing to do with his moral fiber or religious convictions. What restrains the male from forcing himself on every female that strikes his fancy, is the discipline that he has received from his parents, religion, society at large, the law and the unwillingness of females to submit. This is the way it has been since the beginning of time; the male constantly searching for willing females and in most encounters frustrated by their rejection. At least that was the pattern in America until the end of the 1960s. During the end of that decade, feminist obsessed with their demands for total equality with men, challenged what they regarded as a double sexual standard and joined in a sexual revolution.

Suddenly men, to their surprise, found that many women were not only willing, but also eager to have sex out of wedlock. What women called liberation, men called ecstasy. Now they could have unlimited sex with a variety of female partners without any permanent commitments. In fact, men found that it was comparatively easy to dupe women into living with them for protracted periods of time without any legal entanglements. Now, the American male had it all! Not only could he have female companionship and sex without marriage, but once married, he had for a lifetime someone to share with him the financial burden of their household. In addition, these so called liberated women were even demanding that they not have children in the early years of their marriage, so that it would not interfere with their careers and life styles. Just what did the males have to do to acquire all these benefits? Why, all they had to do was to support the female liberation movement, and give up some of their male dominance. Men feigned surprise, protested little, winked at each other and eagerly joined the revolution.

Until the post war years, working men took their paychecks home on Friday nights and turned them over to their wives. No one can despute the fact, that there were some men who squandered much of their pay on alcohol, gambling and other women. That there were also those skinflints who would dole out pittance to their wives to manage the household and those misers who demanded that their families do without, so that the money they earned could be squirreled away for another day, which never came. These situations, as they do today, exist in every society, but these are abnormal situations that are found in a percentage of all human relationships.

These aberrations are not the common and usual ones. Most women expected and were given, their husband's paycheck soon after he received it. In the average household, bills and financial obligations were usually paid in cash. After meeting their financial responsibilities, most married couples had little remaining to bank. Therefore, checking accounts were not readily available to the average person, since a minimum on deposit was necessary in order to maintain one. The chore of paying bills was performed by women, who had the time to go in person to the utility companies, mortgage companies, rental offices, department and grocery stores. The breadman and milkman were paid at the door. Men in more affluent and professional occupations, usually had banking and checking accounts. Many in these situations, paid their bills every month by check. Since the courts for many years did not recognize a married women as the legal head of the household, who could make or resolve contractual commitments, the husband usually reviewed the household accounts with his wife and then wrote and mailed out the checks in payment.

In most families there was a partnership between husband and wife to make budgets and allocate the family income as they both agreed was wise. Some wives had little interest or aptitude for household finances, and in these situations, the husband solely took charge of these responsibilities. In other marriages, the husband had little inclination or ability to perform these functions, and his wife made all the financial decisions while the husband merely agreed, and where appropriate, signed the checks. Regardless of whom took the responsibility for the financial solvency of the household, most married couples agreed that whatever the head of the household earned would be used for the benefit of all. The ability of a husband and wife to meet all their financial obligations was paramount to the emotional stability and welfare of the family. If a wife spent her husband's earnings frivolously or unwisely, or a husband squandered his earnings or did not earn enough to support his wife and children, this usually resulted in a family crisis. During times of economic strife, the ability of a wife to provide for her family on what her husband could earn, was very often all that stood between them and deprivation. The ingenuity of many mothers and wives in their effort to stretch the meager family income during the Great Depression, is legend in the annals of American folklore. Many dishes, cuts of meat, and poultry were until the present generation, still called, "depression food." This camaraderie of a family is what kept the family strong for many generations.

Problems of a financial nature, unfortunately, has also frequently been a major reason for marital strife. With the increase of married women in full time employment, these traditional patterns in the distribution of family income changed dramatically. Some husbands felt that because they were now members of a two-income family, this entitled them to keep part of what they earned and use it independently. On the other hand, many wives believed that it was the male's duty to provide for the family. These women were of the opinion that a working wife was required to supplement her spouse's income only when necessary, and keep the remainder for herself. In addition, many women had an alternative motive for not contributing their entire income to the support of their family. They felt that they should regularly keep some of their earnings to provide themselves with financial independence in case the marriage failed. These conflicts frequently led to family disharmony, causing division between spouses instead of unity. What was once ours, became his and hers. What was once the merging of two into one, became the philosophy of yours and mine. In many households there was no longer a marriage in the true sense of the word, instead, in its place were two people living together with their individual incomes, making independent financial decisions which were often in competition with one another. Quite often, when a divorce occurred, the parties involved were more concerned with the ownership of their separate possessions than the custody of their children.

The campaign mounted by American women to change their traditional roles, has not led to the results that they had envisioned. Instead of liberating women, these changes have only served to encourage husbands to transfer to their wives some of their own burdens. This has very often resulted in women acquiring additional responsibilities, and in turn has caused many married women to perform not only their traditional roles, but also those of their husbands.

The feminine quest for liberation in all things, has led to a sexual revolution in which women freely engage in sex with men, without receiving anything in return. Sexual favors for pleasure alone may be temporarily gratifying, but it most often does not lead to permanent relationships. Men as a rule, sample the sexual abilities of many partners not in search of a wife, but for self gratification. On the other hand, in spite of what some modern women pretend, (unless they are truly promiscuous), most do not engage in sexual activity only for instant gratification. Instead, submission is most often given as an expression of love, with the hope of a long time commitment. The old proverb," no one wants to buy the cow, if they can get the milk for nothing," still best expresses the disappointing results that most women experience in a noncommittal love arrangement. In addition, by perverting their liberties the female has lost the traditional protection and respect once held for them by the male.

Those ethnic groups in our society that stemmed from Latin origins, behaved according to their Roman heritage that prescribed that the male was the guardian of the chastity and safety of the female members of his family. This duty was so ingrained in their tradition, that even the laws of many Latin nations recognized the right of a man to inflict battery, or even death, upon another male threatening to molest, seduce or force himself upon any women in his care.

Those men whose ancestry originated in the Anglo-Saxon nations, adhered to a male code which stemmed from the days of knighthood and the Laws of Chivalry. It was the traditional belief of those from this society, that women were fragile and meek and it was the duty of every male to protect them from harm, seduction and the crudeness of a man's world.

The new culture that evolved with the development of this nation drew from both these Old World codes of behavior. The resulting product was an American code in which women were viewed as in need of special treatment. This bequeathed the newly emerging American women with a legacy of courtesies and social privileges that were guaranteed by the code of conduct of the newly emerging American male. This new code of feminine behavior was not as restricting as that of the Latin tradition. Yet it was not as liberal as it might have been, since it soon fell under the influence of the Victorian period. The outcome was that women entered the modern age with social liberties never before enjoyed by them, which were accepted by the male members of their society and the Law.

In the American society of the 1800s, and early part of the 1900s, men offered women their seats, took their hats off in elevators when women were present, walked on the street side of the sidewalk when walking with them, stood up, if seated, when approached by them, tipped their hats to women when passing them on the street, opened doors for them, always helped a damsel in distress, never cursed nor used foul language or obscenities in their presence, paid for all expenses incurred when accompanying women, and protected all women from abuse from other males in the same manner that they would their own mother or sister. In return, women acted in a manner that entitled them to be treated in this delicate manner. Those women who were crude and vulgar quickly lost the respect and protection of the other males.

In this type of society, molestation and violent crimes against all women young or old were not very common. In Latin communities, a male thought twice before offending or taking advantage of women, lest he have to answer to the female's father, brothers, or other interested male parties. Masculine retribution could be more severe and swift than that of the judicial system. In other communities, women were careful not to allow themselves to be in dangerous or compromising situations, and were usually accompanied by a male if going to unfamiliar places. Men were quick to come to the defense of any women who were threatened, and the Law took a dim view of those males who posed as a danger to the safety of women.

When women abandoned their traditional feminine roles and perverted their newly acquire liberties, they lost the respect of the male and quelled their natural masculine instincts to protect them. In their zeal to convince American society that they were erroneous in their view that women were fragile in nature, women also inadvertently convinced men that they were no longer in need of their protection, nor worthy of their special courtesies and considerations. Consequently, in our nation today, women are abandoned to the dangers of preying males, without any natural physical attributes of their own to protect themselves, nor traditional masculine protection. They must endure vulgarities and other abusive and obscene insults directed towards them, in silence, and suffer these indignities without requital. This forsaking of the guardianship of the welfare of women and the lack of vigilance on the part of men, has encouraged those who would victimize women to do so with impunity. In contemporary American society, women are regularly brutalized, raped and murdered with little danger of any masculine retaliation. Unfortunately, it's not only the mature women who fall victim to these crimes, but also innocent children and young girls. Today, there is only the fear of criminal persecution remaining as a deterrent against these inhumane crimes. Inasmuch, as violence against women is listed as the most frequent crime that is unreported to law enforcement agencies, and male retribution is no longer a part of the American behavioral code, it appears that in many instances there is no effective deterrent to the commission of these crimes. The result is, that frequently the rapist and child molesters need not fear punishment for their offenses.

What profits a woman if she gains liberation from all that she professes restrains her, and must live in fear and insecurity in a society where she must stand alone against the designs of those male predators who seek to violate her?

CHAPTER V

Until the 1960s, the United States of America was one of the most moral and righteous nations in the world. Its citizens were dedicated to a life style of decency, devoid of obscenities, vulgarities, profanities and the propagation of thoughts and words which glorified violence, cruelty, immorality and sexual perversion. In the newly created fields of cinema and later television, it was recognized early in the development of these highly visual medias that they had the capacity to be used as unbridled agents of pornography, violence, profanity and vulgarity.

Therefore, regulatory agencies were established that restricted the use of these highly pictorial means of communication to the tremendous potential they held as instruments of entertainment and education. To this end, in the dawn of the motion pictures industry, attempts to put on these celluloid strips lewd and immoral plots and pornographic scenes was quickly deterred by the establishment of committees that oversaw the end products of this newly created art. The same was true in radio broadcasting, which was much easier to regulate since it involved only auditory communication. The written word, as represented in the book publishing industry, was audited regionally by literary regulatory organizations, and religious and educational institutions. In the literary arts, they were the guardians against those works of literature which instead of being educational, entertaining or cultural, only disseminated immoral and violent concepts among the reading public.

In the beginning, the newly developing television industry was also closely monitored by regulatory agencies, since it was a very pervasive auditory and visual media which could be beamed directly into every home.

In the 1960s, at the same time that television became a part of every American family's viewing entertainment, there occurred a national obsession with personal rights. Those same associations, unions and congresses that were originally organized to foster civil rights, turned their attention to the making of mischief in the entertainment and communication media. This ultra liberal element of American society saw nothing but violation of personal freedoms in the attempt to regulate these industries. They found a great deal of support in their efforts, by those interests that foresaw fortunes to be made by exploiting the weakness of the human race to taste, "the forbidden fruit." This coalition; one with premeditated intentions of exploitation; the other duped by its own obsession to protect what they imagined was a breach of personal rights, embarked upon a campaign to free these medias from all constraints. They employed the same techniques used by others who would undermine the democratic process; the perversion of our constitutional liberties. This time they perverted the First Amendment to the Constitution. They used the premises that if suppression of free speech was against Constitutional Law, then those media that were a means of human expression also were protected by the First Amendment.

Therefore, they claimed that the regulatory agencies were in reality a form of illegal censorship, and ultimately petitioned the highest courts in the land to allay this alleged injustice. Our legal institutions, whose prime motivation had always been to defend The Constitution, had difficulty in opposing a premises that encouraged the extending of a basic constitutional freedom. To deny it seemed to them a dereliction of their duties, and yet, for them to remove all restraints did not seem proper either. Therefore, they tried to take a middle course, which invoked from our judicial system the concept of, "redeeming qualities or values." They denied the right for regulatory agencies to have the power to be the sole judge of what was undesirable in these medias, but did not determine definitively what constituted offensive material. The result of these legal decisions undermined the ability of the regulatory agencies to properly restrain those productions that were truly lewd, vulgar and pornographic. Inasmuch as the media could manage to comply with the nebulous doctrine of, "redeeming qualities," in almost all instances except hard core pornography, they had little difficulty in meeting this criteria as a basis for what was inoffensive. Consequently, this left much of the perimeters of what could or should not be seen and heard in these medias to be fixed by the industries that produced them. In essence, this was like asking the fox to guard the hen house.

It did not take long for the motion picture industry to test the waters of bad taste and immorality. They decided to gauge the degree of the public's commitment to decency with a foreign film called, I Am Curious, Yellow, in which, for the first time, frontal nudity and implicit sexual activity was shown to a mixed public audience. The keepers of the nation's morality were outraged. In some cities attempts were made to ban this movie, only to have this action overturned by the courts which alleged that this was illegal censorship because the film was considered to have redeeming educational and cultural values. The public, however, made the final decision. Instead of staying home in protest to this corruption of the public's morals; people turned out in droves. In the large cities, lines outside the movie theaters ran for blocks, and men and women stood up for hours waiting to get in and find a seat.

This was the beginning of the end for the high degree of decency and morality which existed in the United States of America. Another liberty had been perverted! Thus it came to pass, that those who would profit most by these corrupting and indecent films, television presentations, magazines, books, sexual equipment and lingerie, and those misguided libertines who could not distinguish the difference between unbridled freedom and perversion, convinced a large portion of the American people that they were now free to see and hear those things that had been denied to them unconstitutionally.

Suddenly in America, there was an outpouring of pornography, vulgarity, profanity and obscenity, like no nation had ever experienced before. Magazines, with page after page of women in frontal nudity, or in positions that showed their genitals to better advantage, appeared on every newsstand. The mail was flooded with unsolicited brochures advertising pornographic magazines, glossy photographs, hard core pornographic films and pictorial magazines, and erotic books. What at one time was only seen at illegal men's "smokers," was now playing at the corner adult theater. One had to be careful when opening the daily mail, that a brochure picturing a color photo of an erected penis or a female genitalia did not suddenly appear into view.

How could America, such a moral, decent nation succumb to this frenzy of voyeurism without revulsion? The answer lies in the fact that Americans were conditioned to these changes by other events, long before this onslaught occurred. In any society, if practices that were once taboo are allowed to become commonplace, it's much easier for more radical changes in these practices to be accepted when they do occur. This is what happened with nudity in America.

Before the discovery of the New World, women in Western cultures had for generations exposed varying amounts of their bosoms. Necklines rose or fell as fashions dictated, more or less cleavage was shown, but the exposing of a woman above the ankle was against all rules of propriety. When America was discovered and new nations established, this custom was still an established standard of behavior. In the 1920s, women in our country began to expose small parts of their anatomy in their swimsuits. By the 1930s, the partial exposure of women's legs in silk stockings made the total exposure of the female legs in swimming apparel with short skirts more easily acceptable. The cinema, which was the main entertainment media in the 1940s and 50s, made the viewing of women in tights and exposed legs so commonplace, that female public bathing suits without skirts and even with exposed midriffs, did not seem so immodest. Now that this barrier had been crossed, the most radical of all exposures of the female body could be dared.

In the 1960s, the bikini bathing suit was first introduced as swim wear to the American women. When pictures of this apparel, or lack of it, was first seen being worn on European beaches, the American public was shocked. They were sure that if this article of beach wear was ever introduced into this country, no decent woman would wear one in public. The American people, however, were already desensitized to the shock of female nudity. Soon, many American women were also wearing bikini swimsuits, that became briefer every year. The wearing of this form of swimming apparel, however, was not limited only to mature women. Soon young girls and little children were dressed in them by their mothers, because they looked so cute. It was not long before a large number of American women and children were walking around a great deal of the time, during the warm months, almost totally exposed. This led to the loss of modesty among a large portion of American women. With immodesty invariable comes the loosening of public morals. So it was not so surprising to find that Americans so easily embraced the viewing of erotic, pornographic and sexually perverted material.

It appears to be a human trait that draws men and women to invariably attempt to put into practice those things that they have viewed, read, or heard about. So it logically followed, that after watching a great deal of unorthodox sexual activity, and the naked female form in provocative positions, that a large number of men and women were eager to experiment with varying forms of sexual activity. What was once considered perverted sexual acts, which were unspeakable and not practiced by normal men and women, were now commonplace activity which could be seen in the cinema, on television, and read about in books. Instead of the public going to the clergy for advice pertaining to these new moral choices, they went to the scientific community as had become the new vogue in modern America. These people of science, the psychologists and psychiatrists, had been convinced for a number of years that many emotional and mental problems were the result of sexual conflicts. They, therefore, were only too willing to sanction the performance of any sex act performed between two consenting adults as normal.

Suddenly, books on sexual techniques appeared everywhere, and were even serialized in the daily newspapers. The public could not believe what they read in the newspapers, or in the book stores. Titles such as, The Joy Of Sex, and, All You Wanted To Know About Sex, But Were Afraid To Ask! were best sellers. The viewing public was even more greatly shocked by what was seen and heard on television and radio talk shows. These shows had sex therapists, and specialists in humane sexuality, that not only condoned every perverted sex act imaginable, but were also willing to give all the explicit sexual details concerning their proper performance.

The result was, that a large number of sexually active persons were suddenly convinced that they had not been getting the most out of their sex life. Many bought these books and manuals that instructed them how to perform the different sex acts. They soon discovered, that one would have to be a contortionist or an acrobat to perform a great portion of these sexual activities. Others found that even if they did manage to get into some of these positions, sexual intercourse was either impossible or uncomfortable. Some partners were cajoled, and others halfheartedly took part in some of these unnatural sexual practices, only to find them to be repugnant and totally un-enjoyable. There were also many persons who refused to practice none but the orthodox methods of sexual activity. Those sex partners who agreed upon what sex practices they found enjoyable and what they did not, had no difficulty. Those couples, however, who could not agree, experienced a great deal of conflict and unhappiness. While others, whose partners resisted their unorthodox sexual activities, felt cheated. These either continued to be dissatisfied with their sex life or experimented with other partners.

Here again we see the perversion of a liberty. Freedom of speech was overextended to include the concept that this liberty should not be restrained in any, and all, aspects of human expression. This absence of all restraints, removed from our society many of the deterrents to the degrading of our standards of human behavior and speech, leading to the abandonment of conformity to those established principles of propriety, good taste, modesty and morality. This in turn, undermined the generally accepted standards of conduct in American society.

With the acceptance of nudity by a large part of the public, it was not long before profanity and obscenities were also tolerated without objection. Words that were at one time uttered only on street corners, in the military, or among the crass and uneducated, were now heard in every movie house and broadcasted into every living room, for all to hear. On the silver screen, where only a few years before the word "damn," had caused a sensation, there now reverberated those profanities and vulgarities that should have offended the ears of any decent human being. Comedians quickly adopted this newly found freedom to be obscene, and performed some of the most profane and offensive dialogues ever witnessed on stage in the history of show business. It was not enough that these performances were given in front of live audiences, those who produced them in addition felt compelled to film these vulgarities and put them on paid cable television. This spawned a new breed of comedians, those whose claim to fame was the four letter word and the recitation of sexual obscenities.

Was the American public shocked and revolted by this onslaught on their morals, virtues, and standards of decency? Did they show their displeasure by staying home from the movie houses in droves? Did they put an end to the vulgar performances on pay television by not subscribing to those cables that carried such material? Did the public show their displeasure by refusing to buy products from those sponsors who purchased commercial time on programs that encouraged these obscenities? Did the theater, nightclub and comedy store audiences refuse to patronize those places which featured perverted sexual and profane comedy? Did the movie patrons shun those productions which featured profanity, pornography, lewdness and obscenities? NO! THEY DID NOT! They allowed these abominations to be televised into their living rooms, where frequently, unsupervised children sat for hours absorbing these immoral and corrupting presentations.

Television producers made a pretense at showing some semblance of responsibility by cautioning parents beforehand about sexually explicit and offensive programs, or made promises to show these films only during nighttime hours. All this of course was merely a farce, since many parents are not at home to supervise their children, let alone what they view on television. In addition, when one takes into consideration the nighttime habits of contemporary children, restricting programs inappropriate for children, to be shown only at eight and nine o'clock at night, is not exactly banishing them to the bewitching hour. None but the very young go to sleep at an early hour anymore, and it has not been unknown for children to turn on the television set late at night after their exhausted parents are fast asleep.

It is not unusual in an American household to have four letter words pervade the air from a nearby television set while the family performs its daily functions. It is not unusual for families to view television presentations in which unmarried men and women are in bed simulating sexual foreplay and intercourse. This has become a part of almost all television programs, regardless of type. In the early days of cinema, when one viewed a "Western," one was always sure to see a cowboy," cut someone off at the pass," say the words, "smile when you say that pardner," and the good guy give chase to the bad guy on horseback. Similarly, the same can be said about most television presentations today. No matter if they are comedies, mysteries, soap operas, epics, historical, detective or crime stories, they are sure to contain the following: You can be certain that a woman will get into bed, half or totally nude, with a male who is always nude from the waist up, and frequently minus his under-drawers. Then you can be certain, that this will be accompanied by heavy breathing, the rolling up of eyes into the head, and the caressing of fingers over a provocative, voluptuous female form. All of this is televised in full color, revealing everything except frontal nudity and views of the genitalia; the female breasts being fair game in today's moral climate. Does anyone complain? Only a minority. Those who do, are usually branded as prudes, old fashioned, out of touch, do-gooders, religious fanatics, interfering busybodies, or ultra-conservatives that are attempting to infringe on the constitutional rights of others.

How often must a male, while viewing television with someone of the opposite sex, such as his mother, daughter, sister or girlfriend, be forced to desperately try to ignore a commercial declaring the value of some brand of sanitary napkin, vaginal tampon, douche or feminine spray. The argument that these are products used, in normal human functions and should not be a cause for embarrassment, is a poor excuse for forcing upon the viewing public articles of personal use that they many find offensive to have displayed in mixed company. There are certainly a number of body functions, which are of so personal a nature, that to advertise them in public is inappropriate. At best, they aid and abet the immodesty which contributes so much to the immorality in our society.

Does anyone protest by boycotting those personal items that are advertised in this manner? NO! In fact, the sale of these products increases. The argument, by the companies who make these products, that they need to advertise in order to sell them, is a feeble excuse. They still have available other more private means of communication to display their wares. The only true motivation they have in preferring television, is for the advantage that is found in the use of a visual aid that can even make hemorrhoids seem fashionable and attractive.

One would think that only frustrated elderly men, rowdy young ones, and loose, fast women would frequent those adult movie houses, nightclubs, comedy stores and theaters where profane, obscene, pornographic, vulgar and sexually perverse entertainment is shown or performed. Nothing could be further from the truth! A trip to any of these places, of so called entertainment, will show an ordinary common variety of people in the audience. The middle aged, the elderly, the young adults, men and women, husbands with their wives, young men with their dates, solitary single women and men. They are all there, viewing and leering with excitement and anticipation, or laughing and applauding as profanities and vulgarities are being hurled at them in increasing crescendo. The men showing no embarrassment or indignation for the obscenities said or performed in front of the women accompanying them. The women laughing, with tears running down their faces, showing no shame or repugnance to the words or deeds that demean the human condition. Everyone finally desensitized to those acts and words that compromise every standard of human behavior, because they have grown to be so commonplace in our society that they have finally become a source of amusement.

Yes, these new rules of conduct are all now protected by the so called new and more modern interpretation of our constitutional rights. In reality, it has all come to pass, because we have allowed these rights to be perverted. The laws of a democratic government are made and enforced to preserve the dignity and the standards of behavior of its citizens. This is what makes a society civilized. When these laws are so over liberalized that they no longer have any restraint, then these standards are diminished, and if not reinstated lead to the production of a society without the observance of any standards of human decency, or the state of barbarism.

The role of legitimate entertainment has always been to invoke a feeling of healthy enjoyment in the viewer. It often took the audience away from the reality of everyday life into fantasies and far away places, and for a little while made them forget the trials of living in the real world. Other presentations, produced emotional responses in the viewers that made them feel empathy or compassion for characters enmeshed in heart rending situations. Many productions had morals or were pleasant to the eyes and ears, others were cultural or educational. Then there were some, that were patriotic or inspirational and influenced the attitude of the public toward their country or religion, others motivated the young to seek certain careers and professions. Last, but not lest, there were the comedies and comedians that made us laugh at ourselves and the world around us, that were performed in good taste and without the loss of dignity.

The world of make believe spun its magic spell by the use of beauty, music, dignity, wholesomeness, culture, moral integrity, and devotion to God and Country.

The illegitimate forms of entertainment; stripteases, pornographic films, radical theater, raunchy nightclub acts peep shows, and acts involving sexual perversion, were usually relegated to the back streets and subcultures of the big cities, or out of the way rural roadhouses. They were quite often one step ahead of the police, or agencies guarding the standards of public decency.

What are the results of these new liberal standards for entertainment? Do we still leave the movie houses, theaters, comedy stores, or our television screens, inspired, or with a sensation of well being, happily humming a catchy tune, feeling that we have had a wonderful, fulfilling experience. Do we continue to feel that we have witnessed something worthwhile, and have learned something that has made us better for what we have viewed? Do we today still truly maintain the sensation that for a little while we had been transported from the everyday humdrum of our lives to some wonderful far away place, or fantasy world, where we have seen and experienced such things of beauty and wonder that we even imagined existed? Do we then return to our world of reality, full of gratitude for the few hours of enjoyment we had received for the price of our admission? Do we leave the scene of our entertainment grateful that we were privileged to have seen enacted some event of great historical, religious, or patriotic significance? Are we often full of awe at having had the opportunity to view great and noted members of the arts such as a singer, dancer, musician, or a symphony or ballet company, so close and intimately, that we almost feel that we could touch them?

What do we feel today, after viewing and listening to the sex and violent actions portrayed on our television and movie screens? Do we still have these same pleasant feelings after perversions are paraded before our eyes, and obscenities and vulgarities and profanities are poured into our ears, all in the name of entertainment? Or, do we now leave these so called places of amusement, feeling depressed, full of anger, lust and hate. Are we now, in truth, more frequently glad to get back to reality, and delighted that what we have just viewed and heard are only make believe? Do we now spend our post entertainment periods trying to forget those awful violent, shocking, macabre, and sexually explicit or perverse portrayals we have just witnessed? What about those who are mentally unbalanced, immature, or impressionable? Do they, after viewing this same material, perhaps leave with a feeling that they must put into practice those things that they have just perceived? Today, instead of leaving places of entertainment humming a melodious tune, or contentedly recalling some pleasant scene of beauty or wonder, audiences are more apt to be dwelling upon some new piece of obscenity they have just witnessed or some new profanity they have just heard.

Our men and women of science are quick to recount that this type of viewing should not do any mental or emotional harm to a normal individual, but they fail to consider that it does no good either. Whatever the members of the human race aspire to, should be for their betterment not detriment! What good is entertainment, if it does not entertain? If it only offends, or teaches acts and practices that normal people would not even think of unless instructed by those who use these new found freedoms to disseminate those perverse and obscene abominations that decent society has, until recently, managed to keep in check in American society.

CHAPTER VI

In a proper functioning democracy, there should be no reason for acts of public disobedience, or remonstrations, in order to address grievances, since real or fancied problems can be addressed at the ballot box. This is one advantage that a free society has over those unstable forms of government where grievances are contested by force of arms, or other forms of violence. In the United States of America, as result of the Revolutionary War for Independence and the Civil War to preserve that union, we were a nation of laws and parliamentary procedure where the constituency brought to the attention of their representatives those problems that the public majority desired to have solved. These issues were then debated and studied until laws or precedents could be established that would resolve them, and at the same time, be acceptable to the governing body and conform with our Constitution. Although this system has served this country well in most situations, it did not do so in the matter of constitutional rights for people of other races.

The end of the Civil War, in spite of the declaration of emancipation, did not solve the relationship between the white and black races, nor did it define what rights black people had after the abolishment of slavery. At best, the public allowed them second class citizenship, and in many parts of this nation the only right they had won was freedom from slavery. The American blacks having been frequently denied access to the ballot box, found it difficult to have their grievances remedied by the democratic process. It was not until after World War II, when the black people in America found leaders that could organize them into a national organizations that could seek methods by which they could establish, once and for all, their constitutional rights. Since in many states they were denied access to the democratic process, they chose to use civil disobedience and passive resistance as their method of bringing to the attention of the public and the government their grievances.

These accumulative actions finally culminated into the civil rights movement, with all of its ramifications, that finally resulted in the passage of civil rights legislature. Although civil rights laws finally set guidelines and insured these rights for this country's minorities, they in addition opened up a Pandora's box for the use of this legislation by many other groups whose grievances were not racial.

Suddenly everyone claimed special civil rights! The elderly declared that they as a group were discriminated against, and that they had certain civil rights which were being violated. Legal organizations decried the discrimination they alleged was being practiced against the mentally ill, and that mentally ill patients also had civil rights that were being abridged while they were committed to mental institutions. In addition women's organizations claimed that their civil rights were being violated, and that they were the victims of sexual discrimination. Then there were those organizations protecting children, that declared children also had civil rights, which were being abused. Homosexuals banned together and demanded that they, as a group, should be considered as members of an alternative life style that too long had been discriminated against. These "Gay," organizations claimed that they also had civil rights which were being violated. Suddenly, civil liberty organizations sprang up to aid those groups that did not have the financial ability to employ legal talent to defend the integrity of their civil rights. With the aid of these organizations, even hardened criminals were made aware of the importance of the preservation of their civil rights.

The civil rights laws were only in their infancy, when the ultra liberal elements of American society began to pervert them. Laws which had been passed in good faith, to insure the rights of racial minorities, were suddenly manipulated and extended to cover groups and situations for which they were never intended. Liberties, that had only recently been defined, had already begun to be perverted.

The use of civil rights laws, to produce changes for which they never were intended, has raised havoc with American society. Now, the elderly could claim age discrimination if they were even asked to retire. They could bring age discrimination suits against their employers if they felt that any change in their employment status was motivated by their age, whether these charges were fanciful or real. The elderly could use their age as a weapon to counter any attempt to limit their occupational capacities whether justified or not. Although in many instances the use of age discrimination laws have helped to allay some of the injustices that have occurred to the elderly at their place of employment, they have at the same time also removed from management and the employer their ability to remove from the work force those individuals who truly can no longer perform their duties because of age and do not realize or admit to it. It has also allowed those employees who are devious, incompetent and slackers to use their age as a shield to deter any justifiable retribution. Age discrimination laws have also confused the issue, in matters where the advanced age of the employee is truly detrimental to his or her welfare in the performance of certain occupational duties. In addition, the truth of the matter is, that in those cases where true age discrimination is used, such as when an applicant is being considered for a job opening, one can rarely prove that another applicant was preferred because of age.

The issue of age has also caused great confusion and injustice in those housing units that restricts the ages of its occupants. The inability of management to be able to retire those of advanced age, has also limited the advancement of younger workers into position of increase responsibility which prepares them for leadership roles in their fields. This is a very important consideration, since life expectancy is increasing and workers are living to a much older age. The absence of vacancies in top echelon positions in an industry, because of the inability to retire those of advanced age, may very well restrict the scope and advancement of that particular field. Having older, mature individuals at the helm may give some organizations a certain measure of stability, but at the same time, it may impede its creativity. Young men dream, but older ones are more apt to keep both feet in the world of reality.

Nowhere else did the perversion of the civil rights laws cause more havoc than in the mental health field. The results of the undermining of the treatment for the mentally ill, by the perverted application of the civil right laws, is still being felt in every large city, as well as in smaller communities, all over the nation. The loss of the right to be able to legally commit the mentally ill for treatment to mental health facilities and institutions, has unleashed on the public thousands of patients suffering from a variety of mental illnesses. Once again, those misguided liberal organizations, that continually mistaken necessary restrain as a violation of personal liberties, have overextended a right in the name of freedom to reach a result for which that right was never intended, without regard for the outcome.

With the use of the civil rights laws, they maneuvered the judiciary system into agreeing that the mentally ill had civil rights which were being abridged when they were being held in a mental facility involuntarily. Previously to this redefinition of the law, if it could be proven that a mentally ill patient could do harm to themselves or others, and did not have the mental capacity to recognize their own need for psychiatric treatment, these individuals could legally be committed to the proper mental facility for treatment. The commitment procedures were uncomplicated and swift in most States, and required only the certification of physicians and permission of the next of kin. In addition, there were also legal means by which the mentally ill could be forced to continue their treatment even after their release from the mental facility. Today, mentally ill patients can only be admitted to psychiatric institutions voluntarily, and if they will not consent, can be forcibly detained only after a petition to the courts and the showing of just cause. The loss of this legal ability to commit and maintain psychiatric patients in mental facilities, led to an outpouring of mentally disturbed people from these institutions into the general public.

In the psychiatric institutions, mentally ill patients while under proper supervision, medication, and in a structured environment, improved and some even appeared almost normal. However, many of these patients were very fragile psychotics or personalities. Once out of the mental facilities, and without supervision, and in competition with the normal everyday world, they soon decompensated and became mentally ill again. A large number of these patients could no longer be tolerated by their families, friends and relatives at home. Those who would not consent to be treated were turned out on the streets to fend for themselves, since they could no longer be involuntarily committed, Others, unable to maintain a normal relationship with their family members without treatment, left home on their own. A large percentage of these decompensated mentally ill people, once away from a structured environment, could neither seek nor find employment. Those who did find jobs were not able to keep them very long, since they could not function in a normal society where it was necessary for them to comply with supervision, and relate to their superiors, co-workers or the general public. Unable to work, without supervision, and not taking their anti-psychotic medication, (backbone of treatment for mental illness today), these individuals invariably became part of America's much talked about street people."

The law enforcement agencies no longer have the right to apprehend the mentally ill and have them legally committed, unless they commit a crime or demonstrate a danger to themselves. Consequently, these poor souls continue to live on the streets, and to constitute a danger to themselves and to others. At best, even when they are no threat, they live in a manner which has become a national disgrace. Those liberal organizations that helped create this national problem are the same ones that are now screaming for help for the "street people." They are now calling for shelters and other economical aid for those that they themselves have caused to be in this present situation. Not satisfied with the mischief they have perpetrated, these liberal elements are now attempting to use sociological solutions to solve what in large part is a medical problem.

One does not pretend that all," street people," have mental or emotional problems, however, it is apparent to anyone who has been among these poor unfortunates, that a very large percentage of them are. This situation in recent years has led to a great number of violent crimes being committed by people who have mental disorders. The law enforcement agencies are helpless in preventing these crimes, since mentally ill people can no longer be held or committed by them until after the crime has been perpetrated, or is in progress. Equally distressing, is the danger that these people present to themselves. All to often, we hear of mentally ill people performing acts of self-mutilation, pouring gasoline on themselves and then setting it on fire, or neglecting their own physical care to the extent that they are in essence acts of self destruction.

Even more ominous, is the presence of those individuals who are mentally ill, but are so deceptive that they can keep their condition hidden until they commit some odious crime or other unpleasant act. The argument that there are still legal means of committing the mentally ill, is transparent indeed. First of all, to have the legal right to commit someone for reason of insanity, after a crime is committed, is like locking the barn door after the horse is stolen. At any rate, the commission of the crime has not helped the mental condition of the perpetrator, and has certainly not been beneficial for the victim. The legal route now open for a concerned individual to commit a relative, or loved one for mental illness, is so tortuous, punctuated with legal fees, that few take it. In addition, the burden of proof that a mentally ill person is a danger to themselves falls on those initiating the action, and one cannot be sure that a naive, or poorly informed member of the judiciary, may not find for the patient. Consequently, many persons that are now afflicted with psychiatric problems, unless they have adequate insight into their own condition and seek help voluntarily, or have relatives who are sufficiently persistent and have enough interest and financial resources to press for their commitment, are on the street today. Many receive no treatment at all, unless they are fortunate enough to live in a state with excellent community health facilities.

Can one in good conscious say, that the use of civil rights laws to release from adequate treatment and supervision those who are too mentally afflicted to realize their need for aid, is in the interest of these disturbed patients? Can anyone capable of rational thought, believe that causing these people to live like animals in the streets is a reasonable price to pay for the sake of some perverse ideology? Does anyone truly believe, that interfering with the proper care of these individuals is in the interest of the public welfare?

In defense of their policies, those organizations dedicated to civil liberties are fond of citing those few outrageous incidents where mentally ill patients have been abused, or those few individuals who were institutionalized for years for conditions that should not have required involuntary commitment. These, however, are relatively few when compared to the hundreds of thousands of psychiatric patients that were well cared for over the years, while committed to a mental facility. In any bureaucratic system, there will always be abuses and acts of incompetence. In the last analysis, however, whatever the shortcomings of a mental health system may be, it certainly is preferably to the deplorable conditions in which many of the mentally ill have been forced to live in today. Can anyone argue, that to be destitute and turned out on the street, at the mercy of the elements and the abuses of others, is a preferable alternative. In addition, can anyone truly maintain that to be mentally ill and without the rationality to take those medications or steps that would relieve the agony of mental aberrations, is a justifiable price for them to pay for the liberty to enjoy those civil liberties that they are not rational enough to even recognize? Can any liberty be more perverted, than those which when forced upon the individual will result in damage to their health and welfare? The over extension of freedoms for the sake of pure ideology alone, without benefit to the individual or public interest, is not only detrimental to both, but a travesty to the dignity of the individual.

The national obsession with civil rights, only added fuel to the women's rights movement which was already overheated. It opened up new issues, one of them concerning the exclusion of women from what had been all male activities. This presented American society with the preposterous demands by women's groups that they should have the right to play on all male sports teams, use male only facilities, and be admitted to clubs, organizations and public facilities, which had been by tradition and good common sense, restricted to men. Once again, there was no consideration given to the difference in physical structure and strength between women and men, the absence of separate locker, shower and toilet facilities, or the moral and sexual problems that would be produced by contact sports between the sexes.

The same was true in the question of employment. Those

excellent reasons why women were not employed in certain occupations, were pushed aside as not relevant. Any attempt to rebut the allegations of the women's rights organizations was met with the outcry of sex discrimination.

American society slowly, but surely, was falling prey to word intimidation. In other non democratic nations, a phenomena of the 20th century was a technique to undermine democratic processes with the use of word labels to put in question the motivations of the opposition. If one wanted to discredit the position of their opponent, one had only to call them a descriptive name and then undertake a decisive campaign to give that word an antisocial or unpatriotic meaning. Then when the opposition voiced its opinion, one could circumvent the issue by calling them that name repeatedly, and put them on the defensive. The outcome usually was, that the opponent was so intent on convincing others that they were not whatever the bad word indicated, that they lost their credibility and the issue. This technique was now employed by the rights movements in America.

At one time, the word, discrimination, was primarily used to indicate discernment by a person who had freedom of judgment or choice. It had the connotation of someone who had the power to make nice distinctions. Since the advent of the civil rights era, this word no longer is used in that context. It is now used for its more odious meanings, which has been continually parroted by the rights movements and the news media. Now it is employed exclusively to indicate persons that are so bigoted, that they would make a distinction in favor of, or against, a person, based solely upon their race, sex, age, or national origin. This word has been shouted and repeated in this context so often to the public, that it has acquired the sole meaning of someone who is totally immoral and despicable. Consequently, it is highly undesirable to be accused of discrimination! To be so called, unless disproved, automatically makes one a bigot, a racist, and other antidemocratic things. This technique works well with American society, since most Americans pride themselves in being very democratic and freedom loving. In addition, the passage of the civil rights laws put the stamp of immorality by our own government on those who did not abide by them.

Therefore, women's rights organizations, like other rights groups, merely sat back and screamed, "discrimination," at any attempt to resolve the issue rationally. Many legislatures and other politically motivated bodies, were greatly intimidated by the threat of having this label pinned on them, and capitulated or gave other political considerations to this hysterical outcry. The result was, the winning of some of the most absurd decisions by women's rights organizations ever conceded before by our democratic system. A number of school and amateur sports programs were forced to admit girls to their teams. Many clubs and organizations, restricted to males only, were forced to give membership to women for no valid reason other than they demanded it. In addition, women won the right to perform jobs which by nature they were never suited to do.

Now that women put themselves in situations where sexual problems were sure to result, they became suddenly aware of their vulnerability and discovered sexual harassment.

Although, this nation is supposed to have a classless society, this does not preclude differences in refinement and gentility between the working classes. In certain industries, the degree of elegance of manners and lack of crudeness exhibited by the work force is in direct proportion to the education needed to perform certain purely physical skills. Occupations in which the strenuousness of the work and the harshness of the environment have traditionally resulted in a womenless work place, where workers are crass and unpolished, cannot be expected to immediately adjust to the restraints of polite society. Law makers frequently ignore natural laws and human tendencies in their attempt to legislate sexual equality. It has always been the differences in the sexes, both physically and emotionally, which have resulted in their separation, and not discrimination, in the sense that this term is used today. Society has always recognized that the male being by nature the sexual aggressor, should not be employed in an occupation where body contact with a female could result, nor women employed with men where body positions or exposure would result in sexual arousal in the male. In addition, it was recognized that when a woman was brought into some all male working environments, many of the males would be distracted from their duties, and the female be subjected to the seducing instincts of the male. It was more often found in the business world and the professions, that men by education, social, and religious disciplines were more apt to conform to the pressures of society and the dictates of the law. Therefore, it was in these occupations that integration of the sexes into the work place was most successful.

Although women can and should have the freedom to work in a variety of occupations, it should also be recognized that there are certain work places were it is not prudent to employ them. Both for the protection of their health and welfare and to avoid exposing them to the crudeness of poorly motivated males. The same should be said of sexual harassment. There are many incidents in the work place where men premeditate the seduction or molestation of female employees under their supervision. Others insist on sexual favors in payment for deserved promotions or preferred scheduling. These male employees deserve to be punished by the laws they have violated. However, it must also be recognized that there are many occupations in which the mixing of the sexes is not feasible, without provoking sexual responses from the male.

In this respect, the right of freedom from sexual harassment for women has also been perverted. In their attempt to overextend this freedom, the ultra liberal elements have succeeded in producing such a broad interpretation of this right, that it has become perverse. To believe that by merely passing legislature one can negate the laws of nature, and remove feeling and drives which fuel the human personality, is not only naive, but a harbinger of difficulties which are sure to arise. Men and women can never participate together in certain sports where contact is so intimate that a male response is sure to follow. Women will never be able to work in certain all male work places where the employees are of a certain crude demeanor, without continuous sexual harassment or intimidation.

These realities, however, will never be accepted by the tyrants in our democratic system; those women who are envious of all male activities. When female citizens in foreign nations, such as in China, Russia or totalitarian societies in Europe, were first seen in newsreels and other news media performing menial, arduous, burdensome work, on the streets, farms, or in smokestack industries, Western society was appalled. Whenever a monarch, dictator, or head of a socialistic government, forced women to participate in these unwomanly like pursuits, freedom loving societies have protested their displeasure. Nevertheless, here in our own nation, the women's rights organizations demand that many of these occupations not suitable for women, be opened to them simply because they are only held by men. They will not even consider that some occupations denied to women are not the result of sex discrimination, but done so for their own safety and welfare. By perverting the civil rights laws of women, these modern day tyrants have not only caused confusion and disruption in the nations work places, but they have demeaned the dignity of American womanhood.

The congregating of exclusively male groups, is a ritual performed even in the most primitive societies. The need for men to occasionally have the opportunity to be in companionship together, without the presence of women, seems to follow some natural law which appears to be an instinct found in most males. Even in western cultures, when families get together, men seem to gather together while women gravitate to the kitchen to enjoy each others company. Regardless of this normal need, women's rights organizations see clubs and establishments restricted only to men as discrimination against women. I suppose that at the present time, women must believe that they have been masculinized to the extent that they can now provide male type companionship to men! It is interesting to find, that those feminists that preach the gospel of the importance for individuals to have, "their own space," are the first to deny this need to men. Why is it that these same organizations that target natural, instinctive, non-threatening activities of the male as worthy of their attention, often ignore those practices which are truly harmful to American society?

In their frenzy to ferret out those groups to which the recently discovered rights of individuals had not yet been assigned, those proponents of the unrestrained liberalization of American society fixed its sights on children.

Not content with disrupting, the containment of the mentally ill, the work place, and the role of the aged as members of the community, these self appointed guardians of our civil liberties next turned their attention to the making of mischief between children and their families and relatives. Rights groups now insisted that this nation's children be assigned liberties consistent with the new broad interpretation of the civil rights laws. Their quest now was to change the age old concept that children were unable to make mature decisions concerning their own well being. They contented that children had the right to have a voice in these deliberations, and if denied this right, the all knowing gurus of this nations liberties would rise up and speak for them. To their horror, parents suddenly found that as the result of the efforts of these liberal elements, their authority had been insidiously usurped, and their children were given the right to ask for and receive contraceptives, pregnancy tests, and advice concerning abortion, without parental consent. In addition, minors were being treated for venereal diseases without the notification of their parents or guardians.

These zealots of civil liberties, even went so far as to encourage children to sue their parents to establish these rights and also provided them with the legal means to do so. Recognizing the need to legitimized their intervention into the rights of parents, these liberal organizations seized upon the new public awareness of sexual molestation of children in our society by parents, relatives, and strangers, as justification for their actions.

Child sex abuse became a popular issue with the news media and daytime television. Daily television talk shows, devoted to the practice of using any subject with sexual connotations as a vehicle to stimulate the erotic appetites of their bored, couch borne audiences, featured child sexual abuse on their programs in order to raise their ratings quickly. Nationally televised talk shows daily devoted entire programs to, rape, incest, sexual abuse of children by fathers, mothers, uncles, teachers, clergy, babysitters and strangers hiding behind every bush. They paraded before their viewing audiences, adult women that were willing to relate the most intimate details of their sexual molestation as children. Everyday some new combination or type of child sexual abuse was shown. They featured women that as children were molested by either their fathers, uncles, mothers, brothers, strangers, ministers, doctors, lawyers or Indian chiefs. When the producers of these talk shows exhausted the victim category, they merely turned to their well honed television rating inventive talents and booked the perpetrators of these immoral and heinous acts against children. Consequently, on our video screens we were now privileged to see reformed child abusers, who as if for some impelling masochistic need, were eager to tell all the world the intimate particulars of their sexual sins. They sat there with their spouses and the children they violated, confessing as if they were attending a sexual abuse anonymous association meeting, divulging all the sordid details of their sick practices. In addition, as if these performances were not sufficiently outrageous and offensive, the talk show hosts prevailed upon the victims to recount the details of these abominable acts in the presence of the perpetrators. As a result of these programs, the public was given the dubious opportunity to learn about all sorts of perverted sexual practices and their terminology, that at one time were only privileged to the medical and psychiatric professions.

The mass saturation of television viewing time devoted to this subject, plus the added efforts of the news media, brought the public awareness of the sexual molestation of children to a fevered pitch.

As a result of having convinced the American people that every child was in jeopardy, there occurred in this nation a child molester inquisition and witch hunt not unlike those seen in Salem, Massachusetts in the late 1600s for witchcraft. One does not make light of, or minimizes the serious implication in the discovery in recent years that we have among us a large number of sexually abused children.

Equally disturbing is the discovery that this abuse may come from family members and strangers, as well as by those members of our society who have always been considered trustworthy and supportive of the family unit. However, to give the public the impression that this practice is so widespread, that every mother with small daughters would be wise to keep an eye on their husband's advances towards them, is not only untrue, but insulting to the parental integrity of the average American male. For those female oracles, who write the advice to the lovelorn columns in the daily newspapers, to suggest that no young female child should climb into a bed on a Sunday morning, or when frightened to tears by a thunderstorm or nightmare, if their father lies there, only adds unfounded fears to an already overwrought public.

This national hysteria has caused an atmosphere in which fathers are fearful of being affectionate to their daughters, because their actions may be misinterpreted as child molestation; the much maligned uncles in our communities are now careful not to pat a beloved niece or nephew on the buttock for fear of being accused of sexual abuse; and grandmothers and grandfathers, seeing a beautiful child in a park or supermarket accompanied by their mother, are fearful of patting the child on the head or saying a few kind words to them, because they may be accused of molesting the child. In day care centers, schools and among those individuals that babysit at home, care must be taken at all times, by anyone in the care of children, that their actions not be construed as sexually abusing those in their care. Recently, a number of child care institutions and entire communities accused of sexually molesting children, after extensive and agonizing investigations, were found to be innocent. There has been a number of cases where babysitters have been arrested by the police, and the life of these young persons completely shattered by false accusation from overly anxious, misinformed parents, and their imaginative, confused children. In addition, this accusation is now often exploited by vindictive young people against parents and authority figures, to punish them for some childish grievance.

Women now frequently use this charge as a weapon against their spouses in divorce cases. They accuse their husbands falsely of child sexual abuse so as to gain exclusive custody of their children. In their zeal to protect children, the judicial system has put many individuals in a vulnerable position, where they can be falsely accused on hearsay and circumstantial evidence without any means of establishing their innocence. In cases of sex abuse where children are physically harmed, there is medical evidence of the crime, and it is only necessary to find and convict the perpetrators.

However, in many cases of alleged sexual abuse in children, someone is charged because of the suspicion of a parent, or the actions and mental attitude of the child. In these cases its only presumed that a crime has been committed. Too often we find that these young children, who are suspected of being abused, are in reality only confirming untrue suspicions in response to leading questions originally asked them by their parents or other adults. These untruths are then reinforced in the child's mind by the actions of others in preparation for the charging of a person with the alleged crime. The use of dolls, and other visual show and tell techniques, in spite of claims by the scientific community, are far from conclusive in establishing that a crime was in fact committed. As a result of the exploitation of these unsubstantiated allegations, as reported by a news media that is more interested in sensational journalism and television ratings than in truth and justice, many persons that have been accused have had their futures and reputations ruined in spite of their innocence.

It would take an individual with an ostrich mentality to deny the presence and increase, of sexual abused children in our society today. However, to give our citizens the impression that their nation is composed mostly of incestuous fathers, perverted uncles and sexually abused children, is a gross distortion of the truth. If one visits the mental health facilities of any large metropolitan city, and observes the large number of sexually molested children and abused mothers being treated there, one would gain that impression. However, what they are seeing is a concentration of these specific victims treated in a specialty clinic and is not a true reflection of the percentage in the general population. Emotionally and mentally afflicted people who prey upon their own or the innocent children of others, are and have been found in all societies at all times. In addition, both, ancient and more contemporary cultures, before the age of enlightenment, have practiced incestuous relationships in order to preserve a lineage, the lack of available females, or the barbaric nature of its males. However, in the evolution of human society, as barbarism gives way to civilization, incestuous relations and sexual abuse tends to deminish.

The uncovering of larger numbers of sexually abused children in own society today, is subtly credited by the media as a reflection of their efforts to bring, "out of the closet," a practice which has been hidden both by the victims and their families to hide the guilt and shame shared mutually by all of them. This explanation is a self-serving device to justify their blatant exploitation of a pathetic human malady for the sake of increase television ratings and their resulting earnings. The fact is, that the communicative arts have discovered the public's morbid curiosity with anything smacking of sexual perversion. Those who think that the television talk shows are motivated in their choice of programming by some noble community spirit to disseminate important public information, are naive indeed.

The increase in the number of sexually abused children seen today, is in direct proportion to the breakdown of our cultural and moral institutions and practices as seen in contemporary America. When there is an erosion in these institutions, then there ensues a reversal in the evolution of human society, and a return to more barbaric or uncivilized practices. In a civilized nation, when propriety and order give way to the loss of respect for authority, rampant pornography and immorality, the worship of sex, ever present nudity, and the abandonment of religious convictions, can one truly be surprised that the abuse of their innocent children both physically and sexually, is becoming more prevalent? The wages of immorality are truly the corruption of all those values that made us decent civilized people, and a return to primitive behavior.

This national awareness of child abuse has been exploited by the rights organizations in an effort to justify their invasion into the sanctity of family unit. They have used this issue in an attempt to discredit the integrity of the American family, for the purpose of showing just cause why children should be given individual civil rights.

It is interesting to note, that the liberal elements that decry the need of these solutions for the problems in our society, never seem to see their own handiwork in the creation of these problems in the first place. Children have always been protected from the abuse and exploitations of others by their parents. In the past, this vigil was kept primarily by mothers, since fathers spent a good deal of their time at work. In today's society, the absence of the mother from the home, a great part of the day, has left these children defenseless. Mothers arise early in the morning and turn over infants or small children into the hands of babysitters and child care centers, thereby entrusting the most precious of all their possessions into the care of individuals that they have only a passing acquaintance. They do not even consider that lurking in that home or institution may be someone who could molest their offspring. Older children come home from school to an empty home. They either remain there unattended, or wander out onto the streets until the return of their parents. The heads of the household show no concern that their children are home defenseless, or worse, that they are on the street exposed to the danger of an attack by anyone who has this inclination. Yet the liberal fractions in our society, those organizations who are clamoring for the need of children's rights to guard them from the abuses of others, are the same ones who have helped create that void which exists in our family unit today.

We do not need separate rights for individual members of the family and laws to enforce them, what we do need is less outside interference! The interdependence between people and their institutions in a civilized society, has the same fragile balance as found in the ecology of our environment. One cannot tinker with one aspect of a well structured society, without causing an undesired effect in another. One cannot disparage order, without causing disorder which if allowed to go on unchecked will lead to utter confusion. So it is with our constitutional rights in America. Many of our liberties have been overextended to the degree that the absence of all restraints has caused them to be perverse, and has led to rights that no longer produce the results for which they were enacted, causing chaos in our society.

The greatest deception perpetrated on American society to-day, is that concerning the homosexual. Contrary to present day assertions, homosexuality is not an, "alternative life style," but an abnormality in human behavior. If one were to attempt to pour food or fluid into one's ear, instead of using the mouth for eating, we would all agree that this is rather abnormal and bizarre behavior. The feeling of hunger in an individual should generate a desire for them to put nourishment into their mouths where there are taste buds, proper moisture, apparatus for mastication, enzymes, and most important of all, the entrance into the alimentary canal. The human body has a specific organ to perform each necessary function. Many instinctual needs and conscious desires are channeled by the mind to the proper organs in our bodies, some of which have outside orifices as an access to them. The use of an orifice for any purpose for which it was not intended, will lead to pathological changes in that organ. Some functions of these organ systems are performed involuntarily, others are under the individual's voluntary control.

If a person deludes himself into believing that he is Napoleon, Julius Caesar, or Jesus Christ, we have no difficulty recognizing that this person is mentally ill. This obvious symptom, plus other manifestations of behavioral abnormality, directs the physician to the correct diagnosis of the mental illness. Once a diagnosis has been established, then an attempt is made by the physician to alleviate, control, or cure the malady.

Why is it then, that this established scientific procedure is not followed by the medical community in the case of the homosexual? Why is homosexuality not recognized for what it really is, both by the medical profession and general public?

In the case of the male homosexual, we have a male who is deluded into believing he is a woman. Not only does he think he is of the female sex, but he adopts female mannerisms and in some cases even grooms himself in the manner of a woman. He, furthermore, deludes himself to the point that his sexual preference turns towards other males. His libido and erotic response are finally reversed to the extent, that any sexual desires he may have are only stimulated by other males. His delusion finally becomes complete and is fixed, and he actively begins to seek sexual gratification by relationships with other males. Any attempt by him to approach a normal male for this gratification, is usually met with physical violence, exploitation, or compromise. Some homosexuals for a variety of psycho dynamic reasons, or because of their desire for male sexual relationships, but at the same time fearful of more aggressive males, may seduce or molest younger males. More often male homosexuals find places where others with their same sexual preference congregate. There they form sexual liaisons with other males.

In his delusion, the homosexual in order to be able to obtain sexual gratification with a partner who does not have the proper organ, uses any orifice into the male partners body that will accommodate him. Using these apertures, which were never meant for sexual use, the homosexual deludes himself into believing that he has performed a perfectly normal sex act with his male partner.

Delusions of belonging to the female sex and male sexual preference, are only two symptoms of the homosexual's pathological personality. With these presenting aberrations there are also a number of other psychological abnormalities, that collectively give these sexually disoriented individuals specific behavioral pattern. This type of mental disorder is frequently characterized by; extreme jealousy and sexual promiscuousness; volatile and explosive behavior towards male lovers and other sexually aggressive homosexuals; a high incidence of sadistic and sexual mutilating violent crimes committed by homosexuals against disloyal male paramours; a high incidence of suicide, neurosis and other emotional problems.

Homosexuality in males does not only lead to other emotional and mental illnesses, but physical ones as well. Their behavioral, neurotic and emotional abnormalities in a society of normal people, tends to produce a high incidence of stress related illnesses. In addition, the use of body orifices not intended for sexual activity for that purpose, causes pathological changes and resulting diseases in those organs. Finally, of paramount importance is the sexual promiscuousness and perverse group sexual activities prevalent among homosexual males, that has resulted in an epidemic of AID infection throughout the homosexual community.

This then is what a homosexual is: a male who thinks he is a female; a male who uses the body orifices of other males for sexual gratification; a male who also has a variety of other mental and emotional abnormalities; a male whose abnormal psycho sexual behavior has lead to serious communicable medical problems of epidemic proportions.

"There are none so blind as those who look but do not see! Homosexuality is an alternative life style? HARDLY! Their behavior by any psychological or psychiatric yardstick, is grossly abnormal. Why is it, that if an individual believes that he is Napoleon, and attempts to drink and eat by pouring these nourishment's into his ear, he is without any reservations considered to be mentally ill? Yet, when a homosexual exhibits essentially the same type of behavior, the scientific community is not sure what it is, and the public allows it to be judged as an, "alternative life style chosen by Gay individuals."

Although one does not condone the acceptance of homosexuals by some religious and political organizations as well as civil rights and liberal groups, one can understand what has led them to take this misguided position. The acceptance of homosexuality by these establishments, is a direct reflection of the sexual permissiveness prevalent in our society today. As indicated before, those practices that are taboo, when made commonplace, gain a certain amount of legitimacy which make it possible for more radical changes to be more easily accepted by that society. The American sexual revolution which made nudity, pornography and perverse sexual practices commonplace and socially acceptable, made homosexuality seem less outrageous. The newly discovered constitutional right for consenting heterosexual adults to use body orifices not meant for sexual relations for that purpose, made this practice appear less loathsome when performed by homosexuals.

With their genius for legitimizing almost any act of immorality by presenting them as a harmless sitcom situation, the television media introduced homosexuality into their programming. At first they portrayed it as a harmless idiosyncrasy in some males, and later homosexuals as just friendly gentle souls who were really very lovable. Once again, those who are adept at taking unacceptable practices and making them sound less offensive by labeling them with innocuous sounding words went into action. No longer would homosexuals be called queers, fagots, homos, fairies etc. Instead they would be called, "Gay!" What a nice name the word gay is. Can anyone dislike a person who is gleeful, jovial, glad, joyous, lighthearted, lively, and abounding in social or other pleasures? Of course not! However, what by any stretch of the imagination does, "Gay," have to do with homosexuality? Homosexuals are none of the above! They are poor tortured, emotionally ill, individuals, that are trapped in a delusion that has altered their entire existence. That has robbed them of all the potential for which they were created. That has stripped from them all of the true male passions and desires fashioned for them by God and nature. It has stolen from them their manhood, their parents the joy of seeing a son develop into a man, and the saddest loss of all; it has taken away from them their role of fatherhood, their only path to immortality.

The joining together of two human beings in a ritual of cohabitation is not primarily for pleasure and companionship! It is for the purpose of procreation so that the perpetuation of the race can continue. In modern American society, this fact seems to have been ignored. Today's youth seem to have a misguided impression that the union between two individuals, whether sanctified or by a do-it-yourself arrangement, has for its primary purpose, sexual gratification with a pleasant compatible companion with the use of the most effective contraceptive method available. In this social philosophy of self-gratification, the natural laws of reproduction are usurped by its own offspring and used by them for their own entertainment, instead of for its true intention. The outcome, however, is not amusing! Too late, this overindulgent generation, of self oriented progeny, discover that youth, the pleasures of the flesh and ownership of material possessions is fleeting in nature, but a home without a loving, dedicated spouse and children is joyless, unfulfilled, unbearably lonely and everlasting.

In this social ideology, the cohabitation of two individuals without the production of offspring is, therefore, not uncommon. As a result, when the alliance of any two members of our society, whether male or female, produce no children, it is not looked upon as being unusual by its other members. In this social climate, it is comparatively easy for homosexuals to call homosexuality an alternative life style and gain public credibility. However, by the laws of God and nature, it remains an abnormality of the gravest proportions.

Homosexuals do not beget! Consequently, because of this inability, there lays, within their society the seed for its own destruction. If homosexuality was widely practiced by any living thing that depends on the union of a male and female to reproduce, that lineage would soon expire. The homosexuals who are their father's only sons, put an end to their father's line. Homosexuals cannot sexually produce any offspring with their homosexual partners, therefore, even the production of a race of homosexuals is impossible. If homosexuality depended only on its ability to reproduce to exist, the practice soon would become extinct. In fact, there is now the possibility that the combination of their inability to beget, and the destructive nature of the AID epidemic, may combine to produce a devastating effect on the future of homosexuality. In nature any form or activity must serve a useful purpose in order for it to be perpetuated. Those which do not, by the natural law of selectivity, soon wither and disappear.

With all this in mind, the next logical question should be, where do all the homosexuals come from to replenish their ranks? They come from the same altered behavior patterns that other psychoses and psycho neuroses come from. They come from some disturbed human emotional process, whose psycho dynamics is still not fully understood. They come, perhaps, from the inability of some individuals to progress from the normal behavioral stage of childhood preference for the same sex, through adolescence to heterosexuality. Is it not ironic, that billions will eventually be spent to fight the epidemic of AID that homosexuality has engendered, and yet neither the public, nor the medical community has shown any interest for funds to mount a campaign to find the cause and cure for this devastating mental illness? As long as society is willing to ignore the root sources of homosexuality and to erroneously accept it as being nothing more than an alternative life style, then its true implications will never be recognized and its victims will continue to live in the limbo that this society has allowed them to create.

The civil rights laws became the perfect vehicle which would allow the homosexuals to finally organize and form a movement which was legitimate in the eyes of the Law. Thereby, perverting another civil liberty! All that it required was for the homosexual community to declare that they were now called, "Gays," and that their sexual preference was not some kind of a mental illness but merely an alternative life style. Once they succeeded in accomplishing this, then they could establish themselves as a minority group and scream, "discrimination," if anyone opposed them, thereby having the full protection of the civil rights laws.

The amazing thing is not only that they succeeded, but that neither the medical community, nor anyone else, questioned their assertions! There was some disapproval on moral and religious grounds, but there was never any legal or political challenge to rebut their allegation of minority status. To the contrary, the judicial system aided and abetted the perversion of our constitutional liberties by protecting the rights of individuals to be homosexuals. This has presented the American public with the inability to protect its citizens from those threats which realistically come from the homosexual community. By adopting the guise of a minority group, this status gives the homosexual community the ability to circumvent these legitimate fears, by charging unfair discrimination and bigotry against any group or individuals making these claims. That same society that would be appalled by the presence of a female in a male rest room, now has easily been duped into believing that homosexuals should be allowed to join the military, teach children, and work in child care centers.

That very same society, where the fashion is to recommend psychological counseling for even a hang nail, now has accepted without a challenge the right of mentally and emotionally ill people to work in sensitive areas where emotional stability and sexual integrity is of the utmost importance. Having given the homosexuals the right to believe that they are women with male sexual preference, our judiciary system does not seem to see the glaring incongruity in now allowing them the civil right of sleeping in the same room with other men and sharing their bathroom facilities! Neither do they recognize the documented tendencies for male homosexuals to sexually molest young boys. For those who question these abnormal sexual inclinations. Let me remind them, of the multitude of young male children sexually abused by adult homosexuals in boarding schools, schoolrooms, rest rooms, cinemas and even in the churches. Although sexual child abuse is not limited to homosexuals alone, their predilection to prey on children of their own sex is. To deny the threat presented to our communities by homosexuals, is equivalent to the allowing of an active 21-year-old heterosexual male to replace a eunuch in a harem.

The liberal elements in our society intoxicated by their new found unrestrained liberties, now believed that as well as choosing the commandments they wish to follow, they also had the civil rights to choose their sex. One can vividly recall the outpouring of homosexual males in their ritual of, "coming out," parades, not too many years ago. The daily television news programs and the major magazines revealed picture, after picture, of large parades of, "gays," in Mardi Gras like atmospheres, made up outrageously to reveal their female preference, while they fondled each others bodies in full view of the cameras. Not satisfied with the performance of these offensive demonstrations, these newly liberated homosexuals next established and frequented homosexual bath houses, where they performed sexual debauchery upon each other with such promiscuity, that they created an epidemic of a fatal communicable disease. Never in any other society, since the Roman Empire, had the world experienced such a degree of unrestrained, abnormal, sexual activity by any group that was legally protected by the laws of that society. One needs no other proof than to consider attentively these occurrences, to reach a conclusion that homosexuality is a mental disease not an elective choice of one's sexual preference.

The public frequently sees on their television screens representatives of the homosexual communities dressed and acting like other males, and are easily duped into believing that after all homosexuals are merely males whose only offensive behavior occurs in the privacy of their bedrooms. This is a deliberate attempt to mislead the majority of the public, whose only knowledge of homosexuality is what they see on their video screens. A trip to any "Gay bar," or homosexual community, will soon reveal the true nature of this psycho-sexual abnormality. One needs only to be in a position where they must work with these neurotic, jealous, volatile personalities, to gauge the true extent of this mental malady.

The homosexual personality can be very deceptive, as evidenced by the number of homosexuals that are successful in the cinema and theater. They are readily accepted by those professions of artistic endeavor where dress and life styles are unorthodox to begin with. The right to be outrageous has always been defended by these fields of the performing arts that have traditionally looked upon pretentiousness as a matter of artistic license. In the real world, however, this fragile make believe concept of life is soon dispelled by stark realities.

This government in its quest for true freedom and equality, should recognize the difference between discrimination and the need to identify and isolate those factors in our society which are the result of mental abnormality. For if they do not, they will give license and credibility to those that use the plea for preservation of their constitutional rights, to prevent themselves from receiving the restraint and treatment that they truly need.

It is a strange phenomena, that the practice of female homosexuality is not looked upon by our society as being as perverted as that between males. One explanation may be, that in any culture where the male is the natural sexual aggressor, the female appears to be the natural target for love making. Therefore, sexual encounters between two females may not seem to be as abnormal as those between male homosexuals. Also, the female devoid of external sexual apparatus, demonstrates less physical aggressiveness during their sexual activity. The fact that women by nature frequently demonstrate their affection for one another by embracing each other and kissing, makes the close intimacy between women appear more natural to society. Then again, the sexual liaison between women seems to have an erotic appeal to the male rather than repugnance, unless it threatens his association with one of the women. Today, when one considers the number of widowed and divorced wives who usually have custody of the children, and make up the major part of one parent households, a solitary female parent is not unusual. Therefore, it is easy to understand, that even lesbian women with children do not seen to intimidate the propriety of the public demeanor. One can also sight the fact that female homosexuals, as a rule, do not seem to demonstrate the type of outrageous behavior exhibited by males of the gay community. Except for their tendency to be masculine in their attire and attitudes, they seem less prone to flaunt their reversed sexuality, than the male homosexuals. Since the feminist movements composed of normally sexual oriented females, also are bent upon copying the male, lesbian masculine tendencies are diluted in the crowd.

However, do not be deceived by these observations. Homosexuality is as devastating in the female form, as it is in the male. Except, perhaps in degree, what has been said concerning the male homosexual, applies also to the female.

One of the most perverted manipulations of the civil rights laws, is that of the so called welfare rights movements. With the onset of the Industrial Revolution, the population of most western nations was no longer distributed across the land in small agrarian communities, but now concentrated in the large industrial cities. There, great masses of people had to live in close quarters in order to work in the large factories and commercial enterprises of that era. In this social arrangement, they became vulnerable to the fluctuations in the nation's economy.

On the farm, when times were bad, at least the people had a roof over their heads and could usually manage to raise and grow food to eat so that the family could exist. With the advent of city dwelling, these safeguards were no longer present. The urbanized citizens now depended on the money from their jobs to pay the rent or mortgage on their homes, and for food and clothing. If they lost their jobs, or work was not available, then they had no means to purchase either. The industrial nations, therefore, saw a need to provide its working class with some sort of aid during these times of financial crisis. The experience undergone by the British, with their debtor's prisons, revealed the futility of treating the financial destitute as criminals. Therefore, the necessity to provide aid to those who were experiencing financial difficulty, because of inability to find work, disability, or widowhood, was evident to these capitalistic societies. In America, since this system provided succor for those in dire need, it was called, "relief."

The purpose for aid to people who were in financial distress, through no fault of their own, was to provide them with temporary assistance until such time that gainful employment was available, or a period of disability was over. It was expected that widowed women, after a period of grief and financial difficulty, would also no longer need aid after they either married again or entered the labor market themselves.

The work ethics of this early period, and the personal pride of most individuals to not be supported by charity, made most people resistant to apply for, "relief," unless absolutely necessary. Those who did accept, were anxious to find employment as soon as possible so that they could be self-supporting. Most recipients of public financial aid expected to receive it for a short period of time, and if jobs did not became available in their present location, went outside the community, and even the state or country to find work. Entire families migrated from one city or state to another to find work.

In the early 1900s, great numbers of people emigrated from one country to others for better economic opportunities, the most popular being the New World. During this period the practice of, "journeyman," was also a means by which craftsmen traveled throughout large territories to find temporary employment during certain seasonal opportunities. It was not unusual for men to be away from home for months and years at a time, so that they could be employed and send money home to support their families.

The period of the great depression in the United States of America, was followed by a wave of socialism. The party in power for most of this post depression era, held fast to a philosophy that believed that the government of the people should not only govern them, but also provide for their every need. With this premises in mind, they went about to put into effect welfare policies which they thought would more realistically aid those in financial need. Not only did they provide financial, but also medical and dental aid as well as rehabilitation programs. Each succeeding administration using the welfare system as a political showcase to prove their concern for the American people, kept increasing the amount of financial aid and added more and more programs to the existing long list. What was originally intended to furnish temporary assistance to the unemployed, terminated in being a welfare system providing succor from the cradle to the grave. Finally, it provided too much. In any society, there are those who will take advantage of governmental generosity for their own personal good. The incorporation into the welfare system programs, such as assistance to unwed mothers, was just an invitation for others to abuse this program.

It was soon found, that those individuals who were already poorly motivated to seek gainful employment and lived a life style in which the bare necessities satisfied their needs, were contented to live their entire lives on the dole. This spawned communities in which lack of family unity and discipline led to generations of welfare recipients who had completely lost their desire to live under any other circumstances. The increase in welfare payments that accompanied the increase in the number of children in a family, only encouraged those who received these benefits to have large families. These welfare communities, finally without any motivation and pride, soon degenerated into large ghettos full of uneducated, untrained, hostile people. This turned large sections of American's urban areas into slums full of decay, filth, crime and disease.

When did welfare cease to be a temporary remedy for the unemployed, and became a lifetime support system for those who are content to live on the bare necessities of life? When did it become a constitutional right? No government owes its citizens an effortless, untaxed living, no matter how meager it is. A nation owes its people the opportunity to earn a living. Any political system has failed if it cannot provide for its citizens the opportunity to find gainful employment, to educate themselves and to better their position in life. It owes its people the OPPORTUNITY! ONLY THE OPPORTUNITY! Nothing more!

Why do the members of the welfare community continue to live in the ghettos in those same areas where for generations there are no jobs? Why do they not, like millions of others in other generations, migrate to other cities and states where there are jobs? Why have they not, if necessary, even emigrate to other nations to find a better life? Why do they continue to live in the rat infested, crime riddled, filth of the inner cities without hope and with loss of dignity? The answer is that its the way of least resistance, it is effortless, it requires no skill, no risk of failure and is predictable. These individuals desire little, get little and are content with little. They at the same time, however, jealously guard against any decrease in the benefits that they receive. They have formed a subculture, in which their credo is; that a welfare recipient must receive as much as possible, for as long as possible, without any interruption or decrease in their benefits. They have learned the technique of making others, who do not belong to their culture, feel guilty and responsible for their plight. Their message to all of us is, that since we accept the premises that we are responsible for their present condition, then we must eternally shoulder the responsible for their "welfare."

Those communities maintained exclusively by governmental subsistence, have now found another ally in their efforts to perpetuation their way of life, civil rights. For one to allege that welfare is protected by the Civil Rights Act, one must believe that either welfare is a constitutional right, or that welfare recipients constitute in themselves a minority group. A case can be made, that if a citizen qualifies under the definition of an individual entitled to welfare, that it is their constitutional right to receive it. However, to claim that an able bodied individual has a right to demand welfare indefinitely, and be supported by the taxes of conscientious hardworking citizens for a life time, is not only erroneous, but incredibly arrogant. Furthermore, minority groups are defined as those of different races, color, age, sex and ethnic background. Nowhere in the civil rights legislation does it indicate citizens of different economic status. Yet welfare organizations, backed by civil liberty advocates, continually attempt to interject civil rights as a bases for their continuing demands. Can anyone deny, that this is an obvious attempt at the perversion of the civil rights laws of this nation? Why is there an assumption in the American culture, that any entitlement program originally initiated by the government for a justifiable purpose, can be adopted by its citizens as a right never to be rescinded, even when the reason for its existence is no longer present, or its abuse makes it no longer supportable?

The answer is in the tyranny that lies within the citizens of this great republic. That unreasonable assertion that citizenship in this great democracy, carries with it a guarantee that the government must provide food, shelter, and the pursuit of happiness to all who hold it. That ingrained, arrogant belief, that all these benefits are a right that the government owes and bequeaths to its citizens merely for being born here. It is a malady that permeates the entire American social structure. It is seen in the attitude of today's children towards their parents. A belief that, because they did not ask to be born, their parents and society at large owes them a living. The labor force who believe that, because they work for a living, they should share in all of the benefits engendered by their labor. The students who believe that, because they desire to go to college, someone should pay for this right that they have mysteriously acquired by being born in a democracy. Those citizens in the field of commerce that believe that, because they are part of a capitalistic democracy, the government must help them when they reach a financial crisis and is obligated to insure that they do not fail. That same brand of tyranny found in those tyrants of the past who believed conversely that, because they ruled, they had the right to use their subjects for their own whims and pleasures, is now found in the common man. In the same manner that tyrants believed that the right to abuse those they ruled came from divine providence, the common man today believes that the right to pervert their liberties is a democratic privilege.

Man is most noble, independent, and full of dignity when he earns his keep by the sweat of his own brow. To be supported totally by the charity and the fruits of the labors of others, demeans the human spirit and makes beggars of those who put forth no effort to help themselves.

Consider the lion, he is most noble when he lives in the wild, hunting for his food, independent of any restraints and the whims of others. There in his free state, he is king of the beasts. Take this same magnificent animal and put him in the circus. Feed him, shelter him, and provide for his every need. Then make him jump through hoops and ride on the backs of elephants to earn his keep. Suddenly he diminishes in stature and is less noble. Finally he will lose his dignity, initiative, independence and spirit. So it is also with the human race. We do not create citizens of dignity, drive and independence when we allow them to live most of their lives on public charity. We do not produce a creative, progessive civilized community when we allow its members to live on the bare necessities of life by acquiescing to their demands. It is not Christian charity when we allow people to intimidate the public conscious into agreeing to their claim that we are responsible for their welfare, when they are in fact able bodied men and women who could lead a productive life. It is unconscionable for the political leaders of our nation, to bribe their constituents into voting for their party by promising to perpetuate a system, that in over 50 years has succeeded in producing nothing greater than some of the worse ghettoes in the world.

A system which has turned portions of a great number of our once great cities into such ruin, filth and citadels of despair, that the devastation even rivals that which befell many great cities of Europe as a consequence of two great wars. The destruction that we had once spared our nation by the defense of our country on foreign soil, we have allowed to take place in these large cities by the hands of our own citizens.

Chapter VII

Of all the alterations and redefinitions pressed upon this nations constitutional rights, none has caused more chaos in the United States of America than those which changed the application of our criminal laws.

In every society, there are those that will not conform to the rules of civilization. It is the deterrent of these elements which makes it possible to create a civilized society. Social development and progress in a community cannot occur until law and order have first been achieved. An excellent example of this process took place in the western part of this country during the turn of the last century. The American West became a vital, productive part of this nation, only after its lawlessness was tamed by strong, fearless lawmen who brought the outlaws to justice and established the rule of law in our vast western territories.

A barbarous Western Europe was turned into civilized communities only after the introduction of law and order by the mighty Roman Empire. With the fall of Rome and its judicial system, however, Europe soon fell into social decay and the Dark Ages. However, like a Phoenix from its ashes, it did rise again during the Renaissance, because of the rebirth of those social institutions which are conducive to the rule of law and order.

Our forefathers, when they settled in this nation, longed for the rule of law to protect them from religious persecution, and from those cruel oppressive elements that they journeyed to a new continent to escape. These founding fathers took special care, when they devised the foundation of our judicial system, to protect the innocent as well as to punish the guilty. To deter lawlessness, a criminal law system must have punishments that fit the crimes, as well as a rights for the accused to defend themselves against the charges. In our criminal law system the burden of proof falls upon the accusers, since the accused is presumed innocent until proven guilty.

Until the 1940s, it had always been presumed that adults were responsible for their own actions, unless they were mentally afflicted, or there were other mitigating circumstances. The guilty were punished according to their crimes, with the protection under the Law that this punishment would not be cruel or unusual, but befitting the offense. Punishment was considered retribution, and rehabilitation was a process that was performed after the sentence was served, not in place of it.

After World War II, a strange new phenomena occurred in this nation. The post war affluence, together with the misguided outcry of some quasi-religious groups; the cinema and television portrayal of good and evil sending the moral message that good Americans were always on the side of good; the civil rights movement and the ensuing civil rights laws; the official position of our government that prejudice and bigotry were immoral and un-American; the espousal of the liberal philosophy by the news media and the most prominent political party of that period; and the steady stream of socialist propaganda that preached that those who had too much were responsible for others having too little; gave the average American a tremendous feeling of guilt. In addition, many Americans having recently survived a long period of economic depression during which they did without for so long, were already self-conscious with their newly found prosperity. In this mental climate, it was not difficult to convince a large section of the public that they were somehow accountable for many of the misfortunes that befell their fellow citizens. Indeed, with the passage of time, they even were convinced that they were also in some way responsible for the alleviation of all of the miseries in the world.

To appease this guilt, many Americans became obsessed with the desire to help solve the problems of the less fortunate. They were easy prey for the liberal establishment, who were waiting in the wings with all types of ultra liberal social solutions. One of the victims of this liberal onslaught was our criminal law system. Eventually, these liberal elements armed with unlimited funds, the creation of their own civil liberties organizations as legal counsel, and the confusion already manifested by the perversion of the civil rights laws set about to liberalize our criminal justice system. The liberal establishment employed as its vehicle to sway the public, the major premises that those who committed crimes were not responsible for their actions. They protested that the blame for the commission of most unlawful acts, stood squarely on the shoulders of the American society at large.

Those who committed crimes, they cried, were themselves victims of a society which had in fact failed them. They held that these crimes were not committed by the accused because they were criminals, but as the result of the failure of society to insure that these poor, unfortunate, individuals were properly raised, fed and educated when they were children. Since a large percentage of the crime problem in this country centered in the inner cities where minority groups lived, those who were determined to liberalize our criminal laws made it a racial issue.

Minorities were characterized as poor individuals terrorized by brutal police actions, which infringed on the rights of these defenseless, underprivileged people. The public awoke to a new view of American justice. They were now subjected to expressions such as, "police brutality, white honky pigs, racial injustice, disenfranchisement, illegal search and seizure, suspect's rights and self-incrimination." No longer was there only the forces of good and evil. Now evil had to be qualified! Was it just plain old fashioned evil, or was it evil arising out of society's failure to deal with the problems of certain groups, that caused them to consequently strike out in reprisal after years of deprivation and suppression?

Was it a crime for the sake of violence, or did the violence have a deeper social meaning? Was the perpetrator a callous, evil individual, or was he, or she, really only trying to make a deeper social statement? Was the crime an antisocial act, or was the poor, impoverished suspect merely performing an act of desperation to produce some, as yet, unrecognized noble result?

Employing the manipulation of public sympathy as their facade, the liberal establishment infected the public and the courts with the," Les Miserables Syndrome," This disease, which is fatal to law and order, is caused by an overdose of pity for the criminals and a complete indifference to the agony of the victims of these crimes and their loved ones. The liberal's scenario is: most criminal acts are committed by poor disenfranchised people; therefore, criminals are not to be blamed for the crimes they commit because, society is really at fault; suspects of a crime must be very carefully treated by law enforcement personnel, and special consideration shown to ensure that their civil rights are not violated. In addition, since these unfortunate, desperate people, who never really had a chance were impoverished, they should be entitled, by some devine right, to adequate legal representation. This legal counsel to be paid for by that same public that these criminals are determined to rob and ravish.

What about the victims? Who compensates them for their losses? Who pays for their hospital bills, when they are torn asunder? If they are unlucky enough to die, who pays for the funeral; who nurtures and supports the families and loved ones they leave behind? Even more important, who pays for the heartbreak, the lost dreams, and the shattered lives, caused by the loss of a mother, a father, a husband or a wife, the result of these violent crimes? Who compensates the victim who is turned into an invalid by someone's criminal behavior? The truth is, that those afflicted with the, "Les Miserables Syndrome," really do not care. Their only concern is, that those who commit crimes have every opportunity to escape punishment. Only in the event that the civil liberties organizations cannot; by the use of changes in the criminal laws; the perverted manipulation of the application of existing laws; or the efforts of the court appointed attorney to free the accused, do they believe that the question of punishment should even be contemplated.

With the assistance of liberal minded politicians and members of the supreme court, a guilt riddled public who were obsessed with the desire to prove to each other that they were good, moral people without prejudice or consumed with vengeance, the proponents of the liberal-social philosophy in America were determined to change the criminal justice system of this country.

The liberal movement in America at last found that their efforts were ready to bear fruit. Although they were unable to attract overwhelming public support, they acquired the next best public response. They had managed to stifle any serious public outcry or outrage by branding any opposition to their efforts as being discriminatory or insensitive to the plight of the poor. In this manner, they succeeded in giving their condemnation of our criminal law system credibility, and the petitioning of the superior and supreme courts to change them, a measure of justification.

As a result, the laws that deterred criminal activity in our nation were drastically changed. This was made possible by the absence of any meaningful public opposition to this outcry for change in the manner in which criminals were apprehended and prosecuted. With the encouragement of the liberal members of the congress and judicial systems, and with the high courts stacked with liberal judges appointed over many years by liberal administrations, the courts finally found in their favor. This was not a victory for justice, but a triumph for all the criminal elements in our society. The results were soon evident.

To comply with restrictions the courts had imposed on our criminal justice system, the law enforcement agencies all over this nation found themselves hamstrung. The capability for them to do their job was made increasingly difficult by the police review boards and new rules and regulations designed to interfere with the ability of the law enforcement personnel to apprehend and convict criminals. The Maranda decision, changes in the search and seizure laws, limitations in the restraint of suspects, the reinterpretation of just cause, and redefinition of police harassment criterion, all greatly curtailed the capacity of the front line law enforcement officers to effectively deal with criminal activity. This led to a decrease in the number of criminals arrested and convicted, even when the suspects were caught in the commission of a crime. With the decrease in crime deterrent came an epidemic of criminal activity all over the nation. The number of crimes as reflected by statistics kept by the FBI and other federal agencies, soon showed an increase in every section of the country.

The difficulties law enforcement agencies had in complying with the changes in the criminal laws, were soon translated into a decrease in the number of suspects brought to trial being convicted. Many of the accused were acquitted on legal technicalities even when their guilt was undeniable. The combination of frequent appeals and lengthy trials, coupled with the tremendous increase in crime, led to the court dockets being so overwhelmed by shear numbers, that for the sake of expediency many cases were settled by the device of plea bargaining. This resulted in the early release of dangerous criminals, and together with early parole and the abbreviation of sentences to alleviate overcrowding in the penal systems, resulted in the perpetuation of the criminal cycle all over again.

Suddenly, the streets of every American city were full of criminals. Crime was rampant, and citizens no longer felt safe on the streets of their own cities and towns. The older citizens were easy prey to criminal activity, and people were mugged in their own neighborhoods. At the onset, most crimes were found in and adjacent to the ghetto areas of the inner cities, but they soon spilled over into the suburbs and affluent areas. The majority of crimes at first involved assault and larceny, or burglary. However, it was not long before violent crimes increased to a never before recorded number.

With the arrival of drugs in our hemisphere, and the open border policy of our government, the United States of America soon became one of the most crime riddled nations in the civilized world. In just a few decades, this nation had been transformed from one of the safest and most law-abiding countries in existence, to a cesspool of criminal activity. Today, it is difficult to find a citizen of this nation who has not been either robbed, assaulted, threatened, harassed or the victim of a violent crime. These crimes are not restricted to only adults and males, but also against innocent children and defenseless women. The number of females of all ages who have been raped has spiraled, the exact number not known, since many violent crimes against women go unreported.

Do the liberals relent when they see the scourge that they have turned loose upon the land. No! They do not! Instead, they prefer to completely ignore the crisis that they have created, and persist in championing the criminals and insuring that all the changes that they have spawned in our criminal law system are enforced. The liberal factions, having no regard for the public's safety, are completely insensitive to the plight of the victims, choosing instead to prevent the punishing of the guilty.

Nowhere has the perversion of American liberties been so clear and evident, than in the undermining of our law enforcement and criminal justice systems. Those of us who remember how our country use to be, never in our wildest dreams could have ever imagined that these changes could happen in America. Yes! It can happen here, and it did happen here! Right here, in our country, our nation, our states our cities and our towns! Oh, and yes, right here in our homes!

All of us must face the fact, that within each of us, whether put there by some satanic force or by an evolutionary process, are the seeds of evil. We all have within us the forces of greed, jealousy, hate, anger, lust and the urge to assault, maim or kill. All of us envy and covet those possessions others have that are denied to us. The fear of God is what prevents us from putting these urges into action, or being Godless, the fear of retribution by the Law. If there is neither deterrent, then mankind will give in to their compulsions, and only those who are strong enough to defend themselves and their loved ones from the onslaught will survive. In which case we will have then returned to the jungle!

What good is independence from tyranny in government, if we are all threatened by a even greater tyranny present when the criminal elements of our citizenry are allowed to run amuck. In a society were the fear of God is discouraged and justice is impeded, we may pursue happiness, but we cannot attain it. We have all become victims of a vocal minority, that with the techniques learned from other atheistic societies, and the use of modern day unrestricted methods of mass communication, succeeded in undermining the safety and welfare of all of us.

The perversion of our Laws has not been restricted only to those in criminal justice, but also to other branches of our legal systems. Our appellate court system was devised to make our courts less rigid, so that decisions handed down by judges in lessor courts could be appealed to higher ones, if there was evidence that the verdict was not judicially correct. The appellate system was not designed so that clever lawyers could use them to frustrate the wheels of justice. Yet everyday, the appeals system is abused in order to keep criminals out of jail, or to buy time for the accused or defendant whether it be a crime or civil action, to further find new legal means to circumvent our legal institutions.

When these systems of legal checks and balances were devised, they were done so with the intention that they would protect the defendant or accused from unfair or legally unsound judiciary decisions. These systems were devised with the belief, that ethical and moral members of the legal profession would never pervert their use in order to tilt the balances of justice in favor of their clients. Today, the universal willingness of attorneys to do so, very often makes it possible for the guilty to avoid being punished for a crime they committed, or to allow wealth and affluence to replace justice so that a defendant can vanquish a legal opponent. Many in the legal profession take the," all is fair in love and war," approach, professing that their first duty is to defend their clients by employing every legal maneuver that it is lawful for them to use. However, our judicial system was devised by men who were morally and ethically bound to the principals of justice adhered to by all men of good faith.

They formulated our legal system on the major premises that members of the legal profession were moral men searching for justice, and not loopholes that would allow them to circumvent the law. Consequently, they did not foresee that those provisions in the law which were created to protect the innocent and injured parties, would be used by members of the legal profession for the wealthy and wards of well funded organizations who could afford multiple appeals, in order to allow their clients to escape justice. Nor, that too many in the legal profession would be willing to cause justice to be dispensed not by moral and ethical standards, but by the lure of wealth and power and political ideology. Here again, we see the perversion of another of our basic liberties. The unrestricted and unrestrained use of our laws for the benefit of those that the law intended to punish, rather than their use for the protection of the innocent, and to redress the grievances of those who have been legally injured.

These are the parts of our judicial system that should be changed. These are the laws that should be redefined, reinterpreted, reassessed, and restructured so that they may conform with the realities of the changing ethical and moral climate in America today. Yet! Do the civil liberties organizations cry out for their revision? Do the liberals in our governments or judicial systems cry out in outrage against this deplorable appellate system which stifles the course of justice. NO! Their outcry is conspicuous by its absence! There is a strange quiet from the sanctuary of the liberals, when voices are raised to speak for true justice, and not for that perverted version of our laws that the liberals want us to believe is social progress. In their philosophy, any change in the law which benefits their views of how our society should be structured, is a just law whether it provides true justice for all the citizens of this nation or not.

The laws of any true democracy should provide a stable form of justice for all its citizens, and not be periodically altered to fit the philosophy of any one ideology which may be in vogue during one particular time in history. If we allow our courts to redefine and reinterpret our constitutional rights repeatedly, in order to try and appease every group and organization in our nation that petitions them to correct what they perceive as an injustice, then we will soon be a nation in which the law benefits groups of minorities and special interests to the detriment of the rest of the nation. In a true democracy, the law should dispense justice for, and protect the welfare, of all its citizens. No nation can be so engrossed in its zeal to appease the views of its minorities, or those of a specific ideology, that it disregards the welfare of the entire nation. There is great danger to our form of government when it responds more favorably to one ideally over another. This nation was founded on its own ideology, and that is the American brand of democracy. Our forefathers fought and died to establish this type of government in this new world. A great deal of thought and work was expended by the founders of our government to establish one that was dedicated to the good of all the people. After much debate and personal consultations among the founders of our democratic government, the Constitution and the Bill of Rights was created to form a more perfect union in order to establish a true democracy.

We should do nothing to change the foundation on which this union was built. I do not believe that there is any one man, or group of men, that can change this order of government to form a more perfect union. No one has the right to tinker with the very essence of our form of government, in order to fit it into an ideology that would benefit any one aspect of our society over another. This nation was not created with the intent of permitting the preference of any one group over another. There was never any intent in the establishing of our government to have a nation in which organized groups would vie with each other for recognition and preferential treatment to the detriment of others. The cornerstone of democracy, "is one nation under God!" One unified nation! One nation in which our founders created this democratic ideology based upon justice for all! Not a nation in which any group, with its own personal interests, could put its welfare above that of the nations. Not a nation in which some factors are so obsessed with their real or imagined grievances, that they would gladly tear all our democratic processes asunder in order to gain some measure of revenge! Not a nation in which women are against men, labor is against management, the young are against the old, the poor are against the rich, and the lean are against the fat.

Not a nation where new immigrants are privileged to gain the economic benefits of this nation, but are not eager to adopt any of the traditions and cultures of their new land, even to the exclusion of learning to speak English and demanding that public instructions be written in their native tongue! Like the tower of Babel, this nation is presently petitioned by the voices of so many special interest groups, who cry out that their causes or needs should supersede those of all others, that no one voice is distinguishable in the clamor. In this chaos, the voice of American democracy is no longer heard.

In a democratic society, all the wishes of its citizenry are not simply adopted by its government, not even if its favored by the majority. If it was not so, then a plebiscite would be held for every decision, and those that had the majority vote would be adopted. Our founding fathers realized that often what was wanted by a large section of the public was not good for the welfare of the entire nation. They therefore, left the decision of what should be considered to the representatives of the people to examine and debate, so that a proper decision could be made. This process was devised to insure that what was adopted was constructive and not destructive and was good for the welfare of all the nation. It was never intended that serious changes would be made in order to appease the convictions of a few, nor that the high courts could reinterpret the Constitution in order to conform to the current vogues or fashions of the times, without consideration as to what its affect would have on the remainder of the nation.

What should be of paramount importance in the consideration of any effort to change or redefine our constitutional rights, is what effect it will have on all the citizens of this nations not on just a few. The danger no longer lies in the denial of these rights, but in the over-extension of these liberties to an extent that they become perverse and counterproductive to our standards as a civilized free people. Our constitutional aim should always be true to those set down by its founders. They should always strive to, "form a more perfect union, establish justice, insure domestic tranquillity , secure the blessings of liberty and forever promote the general welfare." Any changes that have been made in this sacred document for the purpose of appeasing the ideology of any one faction, that does not conform to these aims, is an affront to our nation and makes a mockery of this, the most venerated instrument ever devised to protect the dignity of the human race.

CHAPTER VIII

The British Isles and Western Europe became a hotbed of religious intolerance as a consequence of two major factors; the abuses by the Roman Catholic Church, commencing with the fall of the Roman Empire to the Spanish inquisition; and the rupture of all ties between England and the Holy Catholic See under the reign of Henry VIII, later consummated by the Puritans under the leadership of Oliver Cromwell, The English were intent on eradicating any evidence of the Roman Catholic religion from Britain, while Ireland and part of Scotland were determine to preserve it.

These conditions were further complicated by the Reformation and the advent of Protestantism. The result was not only widespread religious discrimination, but outright persecution of their members. This led to the slaughter of large numbers of confirmed religious believers, such as the Huguenot in France by its Catholic ruler, and the Irish and Scotch Catholics by English Monarchs and Oliver Cromwell. Therefore, the followers of these persecuted religious denominations desired to immigrate to other countries that were more tolerant towards divergent religious views. Furthermore, they were encouraged to do so by governments who wished to be rid of them. Many were forcibly exiled to either those nation's colonial possessions, or other more religious compatible countries.

With the discovery of new continents many religious groups immigrated or were exiled to Australia, Canada or the American colonies. When the English colonies in America rebelled against the British Crown, one of the first freedoms they sought was the right to practice their religion without fear of persecution. With victory over the British finally achieved, the American colonies set out to form a new government which would guarantee certain freedoms for its citizens, one of the foremost being religion. These founders of American democracy were specific in procuring for their citizens the freedom for them to worship God according to their own dictates and beliefs.

It is important to note that although the majority of the people in the colonies at that time were Christians, many which had broken with the Roman Catholic faith, they nevertheless, made no attempt to install Jesus Christ as the main diety of their new nation. They recognized the right for free people to worship God according to their own beliefs. They made no effort to settle old scores by outlawing those religions which had persecuted them in the Old World. Since they were Christians, they established their new government on Christian principles, and the new nation was founded on their belief in God. No one insisted that this new nation be founded on a God as describe by Jesus Christ. The God of the United States of America is a generic God. The God we trust in is everybody's God, no matter how they elect to worship him. The creators of our government insisted on separating Church and State, because they acknowledged the reality that there is a secular aspect to life as well as a religious one.

They recognized that there are areas which can only be governed by man's law, and others which can be done so only by the laws of God. The lessons of the past had taught them that to try to mix the two together only resulted in mischief. Therefore, they decided to render unto the United States Government those things which were secular, and to the church those which were ecclesiastical. However, its government would be a democracy based on a belief in God.

This government would ask God's blessings, to be based on God's commandments, and trust on its guidance to almighty God. All legal oaths, and those of office, would be based on the belief in the sanctity of man's promises to God. Although, it was never the intention of the founders of our country to require that all its citizens believe in God, it is quite evident that with this foundation, democracy works best with those with a strong belief in the almighty. It is, therefore, quite evident, that any oath made by its citizens, whether it be to perform a specific office or swear in legal proceedings, could only have credibility if the witness or candidate believed in God. This requirement necessitated only the belief in God, any God. In no way did it imply, that a citizen would have to be a member of any specific religious denomination. Indeed, it did not even indicate that they had to believe in any religion at all. Agnostics were considered to be as God fearing as members of any organized religious groups. Those, however, who professed to be atheists, although they had a legal right to believe as they did, lost their credibility because they rejected the word of God.

Since a person who did not believe in any supreme deity was not bound to follow any of God's Laws, they were considered spiritually undisciplined, flawed in character, morally suspect, and their word not binding. They could not be persecuted or discriminated against for their lack of belief, however, they were not usually elected into government office or appointed to sensitive or important positions. Although many people in these United States were not religiously inclined, atheism was never widely practiced in this country.

The triad of God, Country and Mom's apple pie, fairly well summed up those things most sacred to the majority of Americans. Through the days of trial during two World Wars, faith in God sustained the American people, as well as those men who fought in battle, The phrase, "there are no atheists in foxholes," signifies the strong belief Americans have in their Creator.

Following World War II, however, with the advent of a permissive society, and the sudden craze for every group to establish their civil rights, it was not long before our freedom of religion was also perverted by the liberal cause. The ultra liberal element of our society, with the aid of their legal arm, now set its sights on eradicating God from our institutions. That which would have been thought impossible just a few decades ago, was accomplished with incredible ease. All it took was the combination of, a highly vocal minority, a complacent public, and a liberally indoctrinated Supreme Court. Before the moral and ethical basis of any government can be perverted, God must first be silenced! Does anyone sincerely believe that Adolf Hitler and the Third Reich could have come to power if all religions were not first eradicated in Germany? Does one truly believe that communism, as practiced in those nations who follow the teachings of Lenin, Marx, Stalin and Mao Tse-tung, could have ever been established unless God was first silenced?

Do you believe that in nations where the fear and belief in God existed, that millions of people could have been allowed to be annihilated without anyone rising in their defense? It is only in a world not illuminated by the goodness and the righteousness of God, that these abominations could be performed. Does anyone believe that in American schools today, crime, brutality, the taking of drugs, and the practicing of all manner of mayhem that can be conjured up by the minds of undisciplined Godless children, would flourish if there still was that strong belief in God! What harm did the teaching of the existence of a generic God and the reading of the Bible do to the school children of America? Or better yet, what has happened in the schools of the United States of America once God was removed from the schoolroom? Oh! what mischief was performed by a few old men, in their black robes, for sitting in our highest court for no other reason than to try to appease the cries of a small minority. It reminds one of a millionaire who wanted to help a million people. Therefore, he decided to give each one of them one dollar. He did not improve the lot of one individual, but in the process he made himself poor!

At a time when discipline, morals and respect for authority was at its lowest level among America's youth, was certainly no time to further erode those rules of conduct which gave support to civilized values, by taking God out of the classroom. When changes of that magnitude are to be made in our nation, they should be measured against what is of value to the greatest of Americans, not just to a small minority. Let us consider what could have happened if the supreme court had ruled otherwise in the O'Hara decision. The answer is not difficult!

It would have been nothing! The word of God would have stayed in the schoolroom and students would have continued to be exposed to the rules and word of God. Whether they wished to follow them or not, was entirely up to them. What was the consequences of prayer being taken out of the classroom? One more good influence was removed from the view of young undisciplined minds. This in turn allowed them the freedom to be influenced unopposed by the immoral, unethical, and violent forces around them, now present because of other changes in our society made by the decisions of that same high court. The judges that sit on the highest court of our judicial system, must recognize that the interpretation of our Constitution is not just an exercise in legal semantics that are subject only to legal prose and jargon, but have behavioral connotations which effect the very basis of our democratic principles and social order. Our laws do not stand alone! They stand on a bedrock of moral and ethical rules of conduct which are the foundation of our civilization.

One cannot undermine them without causing tremors throughout its entire superstructure. In our zeal to produce a totally free uninhibited society in America, do we not run the risk of perverting our liberties to such an extent that we are no longer a civilized nation? Will it eventually come to pass, that our citizens are so liberated that they will be permitted to run nude in the streets shouting vulgarities at each other, and be totally unrestricted by any laws or convention as to the manner in which they should act or speak? In our eagerness to be totally free, would we remove from man and womankind the only restrictions to those undesired human tendencies which are held in check solely by a belief in God? Those self-imposed disciplines that makes us different from all the other living creature on this earth?

What will be the result of these changes on future generations of Americans? How will they be affected by this present obsession with unrestricted freedom in all things? Slowly, but relentlessly, we are stripping from them all the ethical and moral values that has taken thousands of years of civilization to instill within them. Those values that, through the process of trial and error and natural selection, have proven to be those which are most conducive to producing a civilized society out of a state of barbarism. Whether these values and basic laws of civilized human behavior were acquired by us from our own innate understanding of what is good or evil, or given to us by a deity on a mountain top, is not the issue. That these are the rules by which mankind has best been able to coexist as a civilized society is!

It has taken the world community thousands of years of refinement of these basic laws and values to achieve the kind of society best exemplified by western civilization just prior to and after World War II. One would have hoped that the ensuing years would have brought even further perfection. In America, however, the opposite was true. The young, the group most sensitive to changes in basic values, were subject to a most profound reversal of previously held normal standards of behavior. First these children were raised without discipline, and any type of adult suppression was discouraged. Next they were indoctrinated with the belief in their own self-importance, self-gratification, and their right to express their views un-restricted. This produced many young adults and adolescents who had no respect for authority, regardless of whether it was parental, in the schoolroom, or by law enforcement agencies. Not satisfied with this perversion of our basic standards, these liberal elements next caused to be taken out of the classroom the only other deterrent to narcissistic existence; the word of God. What was this monstrous wrong doing that was being perpetrated in our schools? What was this thing that offended the sensitivities of the liberal arm of our society? What was this practice that they alleged undermined our Constitution and unduly influenced our young? Why it was quoting the word of God!

It was that the educational system in this nation had the unmitigated gall to read the Bible, and in some schools, allow for a few minutes of silent prayer during the school day! What would the Atheist in our country think? How could their children continue to go on not believing in any God or religion if they were exposed to such corrupting influences? How could they take serious the more important subjects of sex education, contraceptive advice, abortion and evolution, if their minds were preoccupied by the word of God? It was because, less than one percent of students in that schoolhouse whose parents did not believe in a God, might be exposed to rules and values that could actually make them better human beings.

Now the children of America were not only totally undisciplined and without respect for any form of authority, they were also told that the presence of God and the Bible were inappropriate in the schools. The truth of the matter is, that in any institutions where walls are covered by graffiti spelling out obscenities, whose halls are full of children taking and selling drugs, whose rooms are filled with hostile students who carry weapons, the word of God is sorely needed!

For years the only exposure to a religious concept that many children who came from dysfunctional homes had, was that which they heard from the few minutes of Bible reading during the school day. This at least made them aware that there was an alternative to a life without a belief in a supreme being. A belief that presented a code of living that would not only enrich their lives, but from which they would receive an everlasting reward. Now even that small voice has been silenced. Is the result of the belief in a religion so heinous, that it should be hidden by law from the view of school children? Is a Godless society so superior to one which fosters, love, peace, tolerance, compassion, faith hope and charity?

If an attempt to indoctrinate school children into a specific religion was the aim of our school authorities, then laws to prevent any religious practices in public educational facilities would be justified. The truth is that so called "school prayers," were not even praying in most public schools. A passage from the Old Testament was read either at the start of the school day, or at some appropriate time during school hours. It is interesting to note, that objection to this practice did not even come from non-Christian parents, but from those who did not believe in a God of any kind.

The outlawing of, so called, school prayers is also based upon a perversion of a constitutional concept. When did the choice to not believe in God become a religion unto its self? Certainly, the discrimination against any religion is protected by our constitutional rights. Of what interest is the reading of what is believed to be the word of God, whether it be in schools or not, to those who profess not to believe in God anyhow? How can they be threatened by its presence, if they deny its existence? Unless organized religion attempts to usurp the powers of government, and there is a danger that they may discriminate against Atheists, how are they threatened? After all, the message from the, "Good Book," is ignored by many, even by some who profess to be Christians! Can it not, therefore, also be ignored by those who are Godless to begin with, or if their belief that there is no God so tenuous, that they fear that even a brief encounter between their offspring and the Bible will convert them? Their claim that the reading of the Bible in the schoolroom is contrary to the doctrine of separation of Church and State, is a facade. What those who vehemently oppose it really fear, is that their children may be exposed to new thoughts and concepts that may cause them to challenge the life styles of their parents.

The doctrine of separation of Church and State, is based on the concept that to insure total freedom of the individual, the function and duties of the State cannot be influenced by any organized religious groups. That the members of our government owe their first allegiance to the Constitution and the Bill of Rights, and not to any ecclesiastical concepts. The lessons of history has taught us what occurs when a universal religion is allowed to exercise its authority in the conduct of the affairs of state. One only has to mention the name of Cardinal Richelieu, to conjure up visions of what abuses can occur when the two are intertwined. The Spanish Inquisition is a prime example of what occurs when religious zealots are allowed to share the reins of power. This country was founded by those who had been the recipients of governmental sanctioned religious persecution!

This was the reason why, our forefathers would not allow religion and government to form a partnership and were decisive about their separation. This, however, did in no way mean that American Democracy would not be founded on a foundation of Christianity! This did not mean, that children could not start the day with a reminder that the basis of their education was founded on the Golden Rule and the Ten Commandments! Nor can it be interpreted in any way, that it meant that symbols of Christianity could not be displayed on public property, on the celebration of the birth of the King of Peace. Christianity is not only a religion, it is a program for a decent way of life. Even if it was adopted as a set of rules to guide one through life and its religious connotations ignored it would be advantageous to the adopter rather than detrimental.

If Christianity was taught as a class in basic morality for civilized mankind, rather than reading a few passages from the Bible, it would be of great benefit to young developing minds. To banish it from the classroom as if it was an affront to the morality of children, is not only without basis, but downright ridiculous. Division of church and state means exactly what it says! That no religious organization will have any part in the governing of this republic. Nowhere does it say that the United States of America relinquishes its Christian heritage, and forsakes its pledge that our institutions are based on a convenant with God and the teachings of Jesus Christ. When any practice in this country is vital to the integrity of our institutions, it is folly to ban it, especially when it may be the only influence to help deter the lack of discipline and immorality which surrounds us.

What then are the motives of those who profess not to believe in God, in having God barred from the classroom? The answer can be found by first understanding their personalities. It would not be incorrect to say that Atheists are mavericks, who are so egocentric that they do not wish to be answerable to anyone. They do not desire to have any form of morality forced upon them. They wish to spend free undisciplined lives devoid of any moral rules or form of conduct, except those that are to their approval. In the same manner that the criminal personality is without conscious and guilt, so is the Atheist devoid of a need for the concept of higher authority. Even among primitive society, the need for some form of worship figure is usually present.

There seems to be built into the human psyche the need for something or someone who has the power to intervene in those situations where the human element is powerless. This need seems to be missing in the Atheist. The truth of the matter is, that those who believe in some short of higher authority make better democratic citizens than those mavericks who are raised on an atheistic doctrine. A belief in God seems to produce citizens which are more compatible with our democratic principals. Our constitution urged the separation of church and state, not man and God!

Here again we see the perversion of another basic American

liberty. The over-extension of a freedom to such an degree that it no longer serves the purpose for which it was originally intended. Again we see the result of the over liberalization of one of our basic rights; freedom of religion and separation of church and state. It did not produce that limitation that would deter the interference of church in our government without interfering with the worship of its citizens, as intended by our founding fathers. Instead, by perverting that right, in order to appease a small minority, it over-extended that liberty to the degree that it forced restrictions on the religious freedom of its majority to practice their religion freely without government restriction.

Chapter IX

During the periods of history when nations and empires were ruled by emperors, despots and kings, these early societies were also subject to tributes and taxes. In pre-civilized societies, leaders of the tribes, and later in more structured governments the subordinates to the head of state paid tribute to their leader based either on his arbitrary whim or by some other previously agreed upon arrangement. In turn the common people of these nations were taxed by, these local leaders, the head of state, or both. Taxes frequently were burdensome, excessive, or impoverishing, and were levied by the dictates of their rulers. Usually the more progressive the nation, the more structured and orderly were its methods of taxation. However, those who were taxed had little to say about what was to be taxed, the rate of taxation and its distribution. More often than not, the taxes that filled the royal treasury were used for military adventures or to build great and elaborate edifices as tributes to the greatness of their rulers. When no such desires lay in the royal whim, then large amounts of the state's treasure was squandered on a lavish and opulent life style for the crowned heads and their royal court. The wealth of the nation was frequently not used for the good of the nation and its people, but for the enjoyment and excesses of a few.

As the spirit of freedom, slowly but unrelentlessly changed western society into a family of independent free nations, one of the strongest desires of these new governments was to insure that its citizens would be free from burdensome taxes. It was believed that if the common man could control the collection and use of their taxes, a better life would ensue for all. That freedom from abusive taxes. and their use for the good of the nation, would produce a society free from economic hardship and with the opportunity to create great national works.

In America, the victory of the colonies over the repressive British, made it possible for the founding fathers to devise their own method of taxation which would be fair and for the benefit of its citizens. They regarded the most important aspect of this issue, a system of taxation in which there was true representation by the people. They wanted no taxation without representation. The first Continental Congress (formed in 1781), left the taxing powers to the states, not allowing this new central body to levy taxes nor coin money. This was found to be impractical, since the Continental Congress then remained with little power to govern effectively. Finally, this led to the formation of a Second Continental Congress, also called The Federal Convention of 1787.

The mission of this assembly was to change The Article of Confederation, adopted by the Continental Congress of 1781, into new articles which would give the Federal Government the powers to rule this new nation. Instead of revising these articles, however, the Federal Convention composed and adopted the Constitution, which gave limited powers of taxation to the central government. Taxes were levied mostly on land, property, luxuries, trade and commodities, however, direct taxation without apportionment of the representative population was forbidden. The purpose of these taxes was to support the Armed forces and for the financial needs of the federal government. With the passage of time however, these limited powers were expanded by changes in the Constitution, as well as by the law and its precedents, to include every aspect of the economic wealth of this nation.

The first tax on income, in the western family of nation, was levied in England as a War Revenue Tax, and was in effect during the years of 1798 to 1816. It was adopted as a permanent tax in 1874. In the USA, the first income tax was passed as an emergency measure during the American Civil War in 1864. It was discontinued in 1872. Congress again tried to reinstate the income tax in 1894. However, it was declared unconstitutional and suspended, because it was a direct tax and not apportioned according to representitive population. Nevertheless, the passage of the 16th Amendment in 1913 legally made the income tax part of the federal tax structure. In 1943 legislation to permit the income tax to be deducted from a person's paycheck was passed. With the legalization of this tax, there passed into the hands of the Federal Government the power to control the social destiny of this great nation. The freedom from unwanted taxes, which was so breifly held by the people of this country, was usurped by a growing federal bureaucracy which in time would display as much tyranny as the despots of old. Those who would consider this opinion an over-statement, have only to remember a branch of the federal government called the Internal Revenue Service.

World War I and the Great Depression gave the Federal Government legitimate reasons to use its wide taxing powers, and the resulting revenue for a variety of federal funded programs. However, it also set a precedent for government interference in the affairs of the states, and in the lives of the American people. The Great Depression, which ushered in a political party who based their remedies on a socialistic ideology, forever changed the concept of what taxes can be used for, and their distribution. Previously, when there were problems with the United States economy and its constant changing effect on national prosperity, it was left to the captains of industry, the financiers, and other economic advisers to suggest a remedy. Government only interfered officialy when unfair business practices threatened the public welfare, or stifled the economic progress of its citizens. This usually resulted in the development of laws to stop these unfair practices as exemplified by the enactment of the antitrust laws and fair trade acts, etc. However, as a means of reversing the persistent economic chaos of the late 1900s and the early 1930s, the new party in power set into place solutions not based on sound economic principles, but those embracing socialistic doctrines.

Following World War I, and during the Great Depression, socialistic remedies where suddenly looked upon by many as the answer to a great number of democratic ills. Work programs, such as the NRA and the CCC, etc. were developed as a means of putting large numbers of people back to work. These federal programs used tax money, as well as federal loans, to finance great puplic works, such as dams, electrification of large sections of the country, and the building of roads and bridges. These and other measures, such as farm subsidies, did reverse the direction of the Great Depression. However, whether these measures were a cure for the nations economic ills or just expedient measures whose benefits would be short lived, is difficult to ascertain since World War II suddenly intervened. This war, which generated a need for large quantities of war material and its accessories for this nation as well as its allies, resulted in full national employment. The resulting emergencies gave the federal government total taxing powers and freedom to use its revenue for almost any contingency. The combination of these factors, resulted in such great national prosperity that it put labor in a position to make unheard of demmands on industry.

The result of all this was that once the war was won, and the nation, after a period of recession and a pause to change from wartime products to the manufacture of civilian goods, enjoyed a long period of prosperity. The consequence of all this, was that the central government acquired the ability to tax the wages of this prosperity, and spend this revenue on whatever it could get the congress to agree upon. In this way, our federal government acquired the power that our forefathers never intended it to have. One more freedom had been perverted! The freedom from suppressive taxation. Those who attended the second continental congress, never intended to give this government unrestricted taxing powers, nor to have this revenue used for other than the maintenance of the Armed Forces and the running of the central government.

With the power of unlimited taxation in its grasp, the party which had entrenched itself within the halls of Congress and the White House, now had the ability to solve the ills of capitalist Democracy with socialistic solutions. Their grand design was the redistribution of the national wealth. They intended to first put high rates of taxes on the wealthy and industry, and redistributing these revenues by means of socialistic programs to those who were less fortunate. This liberal party in power, was not satisfied with social equality, it aimed to have economic equality as well. The American people grateful for the success the incumbency had with ending the depression, the conduct of the war and the prosperity they enjoyed, did not protest the new direction its government was taking.

The depression and war eras, as well as the years following them, were marked by great social give-a-way programs. Subsidies on farm commodities were expanded, welfare programs for the poor were instituted and expanded, every congressman made sure that his constituents profited in some way by this windfall. A supplemental retirement program, called Social Security was instituted. This was followed by aid to the schools, cities, colleges and on infinitum.

As was to be expected, it was not very long before taxes on the rich and industry would not pay for this proliferation of government spending. This resulted in the formation and manipulation of tax brackets by the Congress, allowing the federal government to increase taxes on the upper middle class and middle class as well as some in the lower income ranges. The American people were not pleased by these new taxes. However, since they were enjoying a great era of prosperity, they dug deeper into their pockets and paid. After many years of alternations of liberal and conservative administrations, during which time social programs were so entrenched that a congressional majority was not present to reverse them, these programs became entitlements which the special interests reguarded as a constitutional right. During periods, when the national budget could not be balanced by the usage of tax revenue on hand or withholding taxes deducted directly from payrolls and quarterly from independent salaries and profits and investments, the government searched for new things to tax, or increased taxes on those already taxed. Also, since even taxes were not enough to pay for this insatiable socialistic appetite, the government borrowed more and more money to pay for these ever increasing number of progams.

The new American slogan was, spend today and pay tomorrow. Thus was born deficient spending, which created such a national debt, that it stands now poised to engulf us all in a sea of red ink. Finally, a liberal progam labeled by the administration in power as the, "Great Society," further ensnared this country in such a web of financial entangelement that today it threatens the very financial institutions of this great nation. The increase in other taxes, such as in the case of the inheritance tax etc., did little to alleviate the national debt. In fact, in certain situations it caused other problems. As land values increased, when their owners died, large farms had to be sold by their heirs so that they could pay the exorbitant inheritance taxes. This very often caused the loss of significant parcels of rich family owned farm lands to the large agricultural combines, diminishing the number of smaller independent farms, which were owned by families for generations. As federal taxes increased, so did state taxes. These in turn, had to be deducted from the federal taxes in order to prevent double taxation, further diluting federeral revenues. Finally, the combination of high corporative taxes, and the excessive cost of labor, forced many industries to manufacture all or part of its products in foreign countries. This, plus the industrial revitalization of foreign industries, brought about by the Marshall plan, collaborated to open American markets to foreign products.

American labor had priced itself out of the labor market, and the end result was that the competition by foreign products either curtailed or closed many American industries. The U.S. Government remembering the disastrous effect of high tariffs on foreign trade in the past, did nothing to discourage the influx of large amount of foreign products entering this country. We are all aware of the serious effect that these policies have had on the automobile, steel and many more American industries. This has resulted in a decline in American prosperity and in revenues.

In the economic world, when profits fall, either wages decline or the labor force and overhead expenses are cut. In the never never world of the American Federal Government, when revenues fall; they do not curtail the costly social programs and their pork-barrel Roman circus; they instead just keep on borrowing money, and increasing the national debt.

This then, is a perversion of another one of our rights. Again a right has been expanded to the degree that it does not serve the purpose for which it was first initiated. This time it is not a moral issue, but a perversion that threatens the very economic existance of the nation. Whoever gave the United States Government the right to tax for the benefit of economic equality? Where in the Constitution, the Bill of Rights, or any other rules of government, as layed down by our forefathers, do we find the right of the federal, or any other branch of the government, to use taxation as a means of confiscation of wealth from one segment of our society, so that it can be redistributed to another. We can be sure, that our legal establishment will find interpretations and precedents to justify the constitutionality of these measures, however, this clearly was not the intention of those gentlemen that designed our government. The right to be taxed only after representation has been circumvented by subcommittees, comittees, and the personal interests of political parties and its representatives. In this case, those who were elected to represent their constituency, now in reality represent special interests, the perpetuation of their party's powers, and their own personal agenda.

CHAPTER X

Matters of public interest have been presented to the populace in written form since the early days of the Roman Empire, and perhaps even earlier in China. This was first accomplished by posting public notices on the walls outside public buildings, or other public centers of the communities. Later, after the invention of the printing press and the production of cheap paper, the newspaper slowly developed as a means of disseminating imformation to the general public. Since early colonial times, the art of printing developed in America, first in Mexico and later in Cambridge, Massachusetts and Philadelphia, Pennsylvania.

Since newspapers were already an established fact in England, it was logical to expect that they would appear in the American Colonies at an early date. As history has recorded, the early printing and spreading of news by handbills and newspapers had a prominent and important part in the American Revolution against Britain. After the War for Independance was won, and a foundation for a new government was established, the first amendment which was added to The Constitution established the freedom of the press, as well as the freedom of speech and religion.

The Constitution established a free press, so that this public service could disseminate news of importance to the nation. The ethical press was expected to report factual events as true and honest as possible, without interjection of the reporters personal and political views. These personal and political views were to be expressed on the editorial page so that the readers could separate the true facts from opinions as expressed by the editor or others. Our founding fathers acted to establish the difference between freedom of speech and freedom of the press. Freedom of the press establishes the right of the press to report factual events without restriction or pressures brought upon them by the government or other involved parties. Freedom of speech establishes the citizens right to express his personal opinion without restrictions or interferences. Freedom of the press was not established as an instrument to shape and expound private political agenda, or social ideology.

It was established so that the press could report events, political and non-political, truthfully and without embellishment, overtones or suppression, by any interested party or agency of government. It was, as so often stated, to be, "the nation's watch dog." The manipulation, slanting, or omission of news events is not free press, it's propaganda! It is not enlightenment! It is the suppression of others opinions and ideologies and impressions, to the exclusiveness of those of the reporter and his editor. The news media also has the power to distort the facts by acts of omission. It has the ability to suppress other opinions or real facts, by simply ignoring and omitting them from the news reports.

In today's society, dissemination of news is no longer restricted to the written word. The duties of the town crier, put out of vogue by the newspapers, was eventually reclaimed by the radio. Finally, television gave us the ability to see as well as hear and read news. This then has given us an all inclusive term, "The news media." Television has even greater potential in giving us either honest reporting, or the distortion of the truth. It can do so not only by auditory means, but by visual ones as well. The pen alone was mighty indeed, but when it is accompanied by the spoken word and televised pictures, without responsible restrictions, its almost invincible. The American public, in this era of complicated socio-political events and lightning fast communications, must get the largest part of their information from the news media. Very few people have the time, nor the inclination, to read books or periodicals so as to be well informed on economic, social, civil, political or world issues.

Unlike the days when The United States of America was a small agrarian nation, its citizens today are directly involved in many moral and nonpolitical issues as well as those which are political or economic. Therefore, there are impelling reasons why they should be well informed. With the passage of time, increasingly more people receive the major part of their information from the news media, primarily the television. Under these circumstances, its easy to understand how much mischief a non-objective and biased press can make. A media that gives only the opinions of its reporters and editors, or worse yet its owners, then no longer disseminates news. It expounds only its own thoughts and views, and becomes a propaganda organ for its own exclusive self-serving interests. Citizens can only decide on the merits of an issue based on the information they have concerning it. If their conclusions are based on, slanted, untrue and omitted important facts, then the decision reached is not that of the individual, but opinions and views tainted by those who have contrived to force their opinions or ideology on an unsuspecting public.

We see a wide division of forces in The united States of America today. It is not just a political separation of two parties, but two separate and opposing ideologies. These positions have been polarized to the extent that the social structure that each party envisions takes precedent over what is most beneficial, or favored, by the majority of the people. The opposing party is no longer looked upon as the loyal opposition, but as an enemy that is to be thwarted by any existing measures. In view of the ever present television cameras, the most vocal and animated of these organizations find it relatively easy to present their opinions on the nightly televion news.

If the position that both parties take on these issues were equally and objectively reported, then this would be a public service. Unfortunately, presently in our nation the news media is controlled almost exclusively by the proponents of one ideology. Therefore, the major source of information, concerning important events taking place in our country today, is in the control of individuals who only champion one ideology. As a result, important opinions of other individuals, or events that favor the opposing view are slanted, taken out of context, or simply ignored or not reported. In addition, many events are distorted or delayed, so as to give those with the opposing views an important edge.

The United States of America was to have a government in which the views of the majority was to be paramount to the resolution of its problems. Since the onset of the civil rights era, the views of minorities have gradually taken precedence over the majority opinions of the American people. Suddenly, a large number of important problems that face the nation have been labeled as unanswerable to majority decision, because of some nebulous moral law. These are now supposedly amenable only to the propaganda and outspoken demagoguery of groups who form organizations and pretend to speak for all of us. In truth, they speak in most part, only for a very small percentage of this nation's people. Most of those individuals, who make up these organizations, do not have the support of the general public. Unfortunately, these are the views that the news media champions and conspires with, in their attempt to use their high visibility to dupe the American people into believing that theirs are the majority opinions.

Those techniques that governments of non-democratic persuasion use on their suppressed people, are now used by our own free press to enhance the spread of their own idealistic agenda. With their visual misrepresentations, their ability to continuously bombard the public with an issue and their slanted polls, the news media is able to present to the American public a distorted picture of what the issues and the beliefs of the majority really are.

Propaganda methods long ago perfected by other governments to distort the true facts are presently being used by the news media.

They use visual aids to reinforce their positions. Many are deceptive and misleading. With the use of the television screen, they play on the fears, emotions and inborn guilt feelings of the public. They repeat pictures or audio portions of any event so numerously, that it makes a lasting impression on the viewer to the exclusion of other mitigating or important circumstances purposely suppressed or ignored by the media. In addition, the news media use popular sport figures, actors, actresses and famous members of the music industry, to support their ideologies and opinions. Most of these entertainers are not qualified nor fully understand the issues involved.

Nevertheless, they are used to reinforce the public appeal of their positions. These members of the entertainment field, have been only to willing to use their popularity as a platform to support all kinds of liberal philosophies that they feel should be adopted by the people of this nation. Since the majority of them are accustomed to outrageous behavior, what seems immoral and bazaar to others appears normal to them.

These highly vocal, organized groups do not believe in the democratic process, although they are only too willing to use the benefits it provides. They employ unprincipled, outspoken, demagogues whose aims are not to discuss issues, but to drown out any dissent by shouting, screaming and refusing to allow the opposition to state its views. They brand any dissent as racism, discrimination, homophobia, unfair advantages, chauvinism, bigotry, harassment, disenfranchisement, unconstitutional, or an infringement of their first amendment rights. They use the weapons of boycott, non-violent displays, hunger strikes, intimidations, and the defacing of the symbols of their displeasure by using paint, blood, hammering nails in trees, etc. All these events reported and condoned by the news media. A recent tool now employed by the news media, is the instant poll. Most of these are contrived and slanted by the use of statistical and interviewing techniques, so that a preconceived desired result will be produced.

This practice gives added meaning to the quote, "figures do not lie, but liars figure!" How many times has the media determined by polling that the public is of one opinion, only for us to find out later that the majority of telephone calls to the White House by constituents on the same issue are of a different opinion! By the use of these methods the news media can influence the direction of public opinion on many important congressional issues, elections and judicial decisions. The news media has gotten so blatant in its obsession to make the news instead of reporting it, that it now is resorting to out and out fraud. The author is sad to report, that at the time of this writing, a major television network has admitted to the falsification and staging of events on its news film that it reported as being authentic! Another like incident, is still awaiting a court date to judge the allegation that events on a news television program were orchestrated.

Nowhere, is the tyranny of any one group as obvious as in the case of the news media. They use their constitutional rights as a shield to badger, intimidate and pry into the affairs of others. With freedom of the press as their excuse, they commit acts which would be considered as extortion, assault, trespass and invasion of privacy, if practiced by ordinary citizens. They ignore the rights of others and democratic principals, yet jealously guard their own constitutional rights as if they were created by divine intervention. Their arrogance, irreverence, rudeness and lack of sensitivity, is recognized worldwide. They sit in the envied position of criticizing the acts and decisions of others, while they themselves never engage in any activity that can be scrutinized and criticized. They have all the questions, but none of the answers. They are always the inquisitors, but they themselves are never judged. In the entertainment world, they would be known as the no talent group. The problems and mischief created by the news media, in the name of freedom of the press, is incalculable.

Many would say, that the ills of the free press are evenly balance by the good they do by bringing into public view, facts which could easily be hidden if it was not for their ever present vigilance. The truth of the matter is, that the major news sources are no longer the ethical devotees of the truth that they use to be. They are today, more concerned with television ratings, sponsors, subscribers and circulation. They glorify sensationalism and trivialize other less glamorous events. They are afflicted with a short attention span, and yesterdays impelling issues or earth shaking foreign events that they reported with such urgency, are easily forgotten in favor of today's new revelations of impending doom. They delight in prognosticating all types of negative conclusions and temper every evidence of good news by some contradicting qualification.

When the Constitution and The Bill Of Rights were created by our forefathers, they were devised with the intent that these documents would safeguard the freedom of the citizens of this newly formed democracy. In order to insure freedom and to avoid the return of tyranny, the founders of this country not only seeked protection from foreign intervention, but also against the over domination of its citizens by its own government. They seeked to insure that the reins of government would never be so strong, as to dictate to the electorate and compromise their freedoms. For this reason, they wanted to insure the existence of a free press. These men recognizing that as long as the actions of government, and the views of the people, were honestly and without bias reported by a free press, the right hand always new what the left hand was doing. Since that time, a free press has been a basic necessity in the creation and establishing of any democratic government. It is the watchdog of all free nations, but only if approval and decent, acts of praise and villainy are impartially reported, and governments are held accountable for their actions. A free press must be ethical and truthful, if not, it will loose its credibility and the reason for its existence will no longer exist!

The press is an awesome instrument of power. Used correctly, it is the bulwark for the preservation of freedom. Used incorrectly, it forever loses its ability to function as a safeguard against tyranny.

The state of the present day press is another example of the tyranny of the common man, and the perversion of another of our freedoms. It is a clear illustration of how power in the hands of even common men can breed arrogance, deception and corruption, leading to a tyranny of its own.

Again we find a freedom so overextended, that it has lead to the distorted application of its principles, and to its perversion.

Chapter XI

Nowhere, is the decline of American society more evident than in its great cities. What once were symbols of a proud democratic society have now degenerated, in a few decades, into ghettoes of indescribable ruin and decay. It seems as if these once proud structures have mirrored the plight of those unfortunates that live within them. Where once stood beautiful boulevards full of trees and flowers anchored by lush lawns and paths, now is found fallow ground, full of trash, garbage and abandoned rusting vehicles of different varieties. Where once were clean, tree lined streets, now are trash filled gutters and the stump of trees long ago dead because of neglect and abuse.

The large fashionable row houses are now defaced, vandalized and covered with graffiti expressing the hate and vulgarity of the people who lived there. In homes, where once lived one family, now live four or more. Those homes which have been so abused that they are no longer habitable, now lay abandoned. The interiors of these houses gutted out unless fortunate enough to be boarded up by its owner or the city. Those public buildings that have had the misfortune of being located close to these sections, are also covered with graffiti and defaced, and with all of its windows covered by metal screening and bars to keep the vandals out. Many of the street lights no longer function, because either the bulbs have been broken, or the lamp poles have been torn down.

Those public transportation vehicles that cross these areas are also covered by revolting graffiti. The once prosperous business areas lined with little shops and larger stores did not fare any better than the residential areas. The windows in most of the store fronts have been broken and covered over with plywood. Those that remain, in order to protect them, have metal lath-like shades that are drawn every night when the owner leaves the premises. There are a few food stores still opened. These usually are owned either by older proprietors who have been there for years, or newly arrived immigrates who feel that even these danger filled environments hold opportunities previously denied to them in their homelands. Sad to say, there are plenty of bars and liquor stores still present to supply the spirits which fuel violence and vice in this already over abused society. Many homes have been declared condemned by the city, and have been torn down leaving behind empty lots covered with rubbish and debris.

How did all this come about? From the time that people first began favoring the cities as a place to reside, a result of the industrial revolution, there have always been sections of the cities where those with low income and the minorities lived. At first these areas were relatively small. The Civil War resulted in a migration of some of the blacks from the south and increased the size of some of these areas.

The great immigration from Europe also brought to the cities a large number of unskilled low salaried people, who lived in enclaves of ethnic neighborhoods, where they could live with their own countrymen. Most of these progressed steadily into becoming middle class areas. Some did not, and further increased the number of people who lived in substandard houses in crime infested sections. These changes occurred in most of the large cities in the northeast section of the United States. The size of these areas of under privileged people remained more or less stable until World War II. At that time, they made up a relatively small section of the large sprawling northern cities.

The war made it necessary for this country to manufacture a tremendous amount of war material. This led to a need for the large factories, most of them located in the northeast to enlarge their labor force. To fill these needs, especially in the low skilled positions, a large number of workers some just emerging from the effects of the Great Depression migrated to the northeast. In addition, a large number of blacks from the south also moved north to take advantage of the many occupational opportunities. This resulted in a demand for more low income housing close to the factories and to public transportation. The first to be occupied by these defense workers were those small homes adjacent to the factories, which had never been popular in the past. Some were built and subsidized by the adjacent factories. Most had been poorly maintained and were in bad condition. However, since the demand was greater than the supply, many real estate companies and private individuals bought large numbers of these homes, and after making them barely livable, rented them at exorbitant prices.

The number of these houses available were just barely enough to shelter a very small part of the labor force which had migrated to these large cities. Seizing this opportunity to take advantage of the growing need, many large real estate companies searched for large homes that could be converted into multiple family dwellings. They went into well-to-do fashionable neighborhoods and offered to buy homes at more than the market value. Most homeowners resisted. However, they were frequently able to find one or two home owners who could not resist the lure of money. Once these homes were purchased, the real estate agencies using wartime emergency relaxation of zoning laws, converted them into multiple family dwellings. This change in the makeup of the neighborhood, frightened many of the residents resulting in a rash of homes being put up for sale. This further decreased the desirability of living in these neighborhoods, which decreased the real estate value of the properties even more.

In time, many of these single family dwellings were bought at bargain prices, and converted to multiple family dwellings. In the fashionable areas of the city this change resulted in the turning of these homes into apartments for the middle class, which remained stable throughout the war years. However, when this same process occurred in the middle class areas, this change caused many of the residents to flee, retreating from the tide of large numbers of minorities and low income renters. When the war ended, the loss of employment opportunities did not reverse the process, and the people in these communities did not move back to their place of origin. Many found jobs elsewhere and those without transferable skills became welfare recipients. Eventually, the homes which had been turned into middle class apartments, were further changed by the large real estate companies into low income multiple family dwellings.

These low income areas soon were plagued by crime and violence forcing the few remaining middle class residents out of these neighborhoods. These then became ghettoes! It was not long before this crime and violence spilled over into adjacent well maintained sections of the cities, resulting in the well published," white flight," of the city residents to the outlining suburbs.

This then resulted in the division of the cities, as we know them today. An inner city of filth, crime, loss of industry and the deterioration of the human spirit within its citizens. A society without family units, where the males are only interested in satisfying their sexual needs, producing offspring that they neither recognize, rear, nor support. A society made up of mostly women struggling to rear, feed, and educate children who are reared on the street knowing neither discipline, respect, love nor compassion. A battle ground in a war to control the drug traffic. Where innocent children and adults are gunned down by males who have finally reached the same barbarous uncivilized state that they had originated from. It took thousands of years to develop a civilized society, and just a few decades for it to revert to barbarism. A society terrorized by drug addicts and their suppliers, criminals and juvenile gangs. A society that must live behind closed doors to keep out their hostile environment.

The other is the outer city, comprising of people who were tenacious enough to resist the lure of the large real estate inducements; those who where separated from these undesirable sections by some geographic barrier; and those who now live where large areas of adjacent farmland had been transformed into the suburbs. In response to these changes, many industries and businesses soon also moved to the outer city. In a matter of decades, entire cities had moved from their centers out to their periphery so that they could escape the chaos of what were once tranquil, prosperous, beautiful and safe citadels. And so it came to pass, that the outer cities are now the cradles of civilized society, and the inner cities are the caldrons of crime, filth and the symbol of a society without values. If one should ever doubt the need of laws, both God's and man's, to maintain a civilized society, then one has only to look at the inner cities as a model of what evolves when a society has neither.

America has finally been divided into a two tier society, one endowed by all the characteristics of civilized society, the other enclaves of violence, misery and despair. The attempt to solve the problems of the inner cities have met with conflicting motives, resulting in utter chaos and ill feelings. It is truly an enigma. If welfare aid is curtailed, then American society is accused of insensitivity, discrimination and not caring about the plight of the poverty stricken. If welfare aid is increased, then those in office are accused of contributing to the decline in motivation for the depressed to get off the dole. If police activity is increased to protect the innocent, then they are accused of police brutality. If the police take a low profile in these areas, then they are accused of coddling the criminals and shirking their duties. If sociologists suggest that the people in these ghettoes should take responsibility for their own improvement, they are accused of discrimination and bigotry.

The attempt to solve the ghetto's low rent public housing has met with equally dismal failure. Proving the point that ghettoes are made and do not, as some have suggested, appear out of the ground like some giant toadstool! Starting even before World War II, experiments with public housing have taken place in selected states in this country. No matter how well intended and appointed these projects were, they all ended up with the same fate. They were in no time turned into dens of filth, ravaged by neglect and vandalism, and the spawning ground for crime and violence. Today, they have also become centers for drugs and drug trafficking. This is a testimony to the often shunned truth that no segment of society can improve until those involved take interest in bettering themselves. Discipline at home, a predilection for cleanliness, an abhorrence to chaos, filth and disorder, cannot be purchased with government stipends. Fear of God, respect for authority, the love of law and order and the rejection of crime and violence can not be instilled in any society by government programs and the expenditure of billions of dollars. Those qualities which makes a civilized society, need not be purchased for they are there just for the taking!

We do not need unlimited charity and stewardship, what we do need is motivation! We need to make this section of society desire to lead a different type of life. Those who are in charge of solving this problem do not help this down trodden mass by making them content to live a meager existence. It would be better if they had nothing as an incentive to strive for more, than give them just enough to exist so that they do not have the motivation to improve beyond a bare subsistence.

This problem is further aggravated by those leaders of the ghetto society, who make a career out of the frustrations and unfulfilled desires of their rank and file. Instead of encouraging the members of this society to be enterprising, orderly and self-sufficient, they drug them with the bromide of reparations for previous grievances, and the need to arise and strike off the shackles which they claim still bind them. If these leaders were as interested in self-improvement, as they are for providing excuses for the past failures of their community, then maybe some progress can be made. This society does not need a crutch, it needs its own strong arms and steady legs to bring them to that mountain that they so eagerly search for. Here we see, in all its fury, the tyranny that the common man himself can engender. One section demanding that they be allowed special liberties not available to other members of the same society as repayment for previous injustices. At the same time, condoning the crime and violence of its own society as justifiable actions in retaliation for these injustices. America has now been divided into those who have not and blame the rest of society for its own failures, and those who have, and require that those who have not to pull themselves up by their booth straps and stop looking for a handout, refusing to concede that others may have different barriers to overcome than they had.

The minorities believe that government aid is retribution for previous offenses. The political party in control of congress for most of the time since World War II, believe that the government is responsible for their welfare for as long as its necessary. They continuously pass programs to improve the plight of the underprivileged. These programs are based on the major premises that the welfare recipients, that make up most of the population of the inner city, will be trained and educated so that they can find better opportunities. What they fail to realize, is that before these individuals can take advantage of these opportunities, they must first be civilized. They must first gain respect for authoritarian figures, whether they be police, teachers or clergymen. They must first have sufficient pride in themselves to adhere to the disciplines of cleanliness, good grooming and civil decency. You cannot take a hostile, unclean, disheveled person, who cannot relate to others in society, and does not have even the rudiments of a formal education, and elevate them into a well paying occupation. In their present condition, they are only fit for very menial jobs, that at times pay less than they receive from their welfare checks. Today in America, an individual must have sufficient training or education to be able to be employed in a good paying occupation. Many such programs are available. However, it takes hard work and study disciplines to recast an individual into an upstanding productive citizen who is self-supporting and contributing to society instead living off of it.

Meanwhile, this pressing national problem can never be solved as long as its solution is muddled by those liberal social economic theories that are constantly being championed by the liberal elements in our society. Policies which are naive, emotionally attractive, but impractical and unfeasible, and have only made this situation worse. They have, in the most part, all been tried in the past and have met with failure. These policies have only succeeded in turning these problems from social economic ones, into those that have to do with civil rights. The charges of a racial discriminatory conspiracy have only complicated the solutions.

As the ghettoes grow increasingly larger, more and more areas of the large cities lose those residents who contribute to the revenues which pay for its upkeep and the public services. At the same time that a great number of tax paying citizens are loss, an increasing number of residents in these areas join the welfare rolls, and receive not only payments, but in addition all of the free services that go with it. This means that fewer and fewer people remain to pay taxes that support ,the services and care that are given to increasing number of its citizens. Is it no wonder, that many of our large cities are going bankrupt, and large number of essential services for the other citizens are curtailed.

If one is looking for a microcosm of what happens in a society in which there is no restraint, no respect for the law, perversion of its liberties, and without a fear of the almighty, the ghettoes would be an excellent model. Here is true tyranny! Ordinary citizens demanding that its government keep them from the cradle to the grave, because of their color, national origin and past injustices. Here is true perversion of democratic principles: the view that if charity be the credo of Christianity, and this government is founded on the bedrock of that faith, then those who need assistance should not receive only temporary succor, but be carried on the backs of its hard working, independent citizens for a lifetime.

The ghetto is a vivid example of all that can go wrong with a society. It is the end product of the perversion of our liberties and the expression of the tyranny within us. We have seen the results produced by the abandonment of women from their traditional roll in the family unit. Now, in these bastions of human devastation, we are confronted with the results of male abandonment. That frequently results in total dissolution of the family as it exists in all civilized societies. Here we see the results of the altering of those deterrents which makes it possible for ghettoes to develop and persist. Those welfare concepts which allow people to just exist, affording them just sufficient aid so that they have no incentive to better their lot by the sweat of their own brow. They are rewarded for their acquiescence to these policies that allows them to live a marginal life without any hope in its betterment, by accepting the charity of the nation rather then enjoying the fruits of their own labor.

CHAPTER XII

One of the most devastating decisions made by this country, is its present policy on immigration. In the past, immigration into this country was a guarded privilege protected by laws and quotas and subject to scrutiny by both the health and immigration departments. Those individuals who had the most to offer to this new nation were preferred. These immigrants had to demonstrate good health, as well as their desire to eventually be citizens of this country, and that they were not affiliated with foreign governments dedicated to the overthrow of our democratic system of government. This political requirement was more or less taken for granted, since all immigrants prized the opportunity to be an American citizen above all other considerations. The history of what occurred at Ellis Island, New York is too well known to be repeated at this writing. The great immigration from Ireland and Europe during the turn of the century and in the early 1900s, brought to this country, in most part, people of excellent character, determination and talent. Their great desire to become citizens and imitate the life style and customs of our country, quickly made them part of the of the American scene. The great contribution both in labor, as well as in intellectual and artistic pursuits that they gave to this nation, are still clearly visible in our society today.

The small row and semi-detached houses where they had settled and reared their families, have now almost all been abandoned by these early immigrants. They are presently either a part of the inner city, or swallowed up by commercial development or the expansion of roads and highways. Most of the first generation of immigrants have all passed on now, leaving behind for their children a legacy of principles, character and the willingness to work and make sacrifices for the promise of a better life. These then, their children and grandchildren, have inherited the American dream. They now live in desirable places, consistent with their status in our society, and have the positions, professions and occupations which they have earned by hard work and study. That was, in many cases, made possible by their own sacrifices or financial and moral support from their parents or older siblings. Many of them have distinguished themselves not only in the professions, but also in government and as captains of industry. The early immigrants contributed to our nation not only their skills, but in addition themselves, which frequently was the biggest prize of all. These new Americans help build the cities, the railroads, contributed to the wealth of the nation, and willingly sent their children off to war in the defense of their country. They were devoted patriots and supporters of our democratic way of life.

No nation, whether great or small, can long exist without maintaining the integrity of its borders. The United States of America has vast borders, because of its size. Until the end of World War II, this country had little concern with its borders. To the north with Canada, the open border policy supported by well staffed crossing points and a law abiding population easily controlled any illegal immigration. In addition, the geography and weather of a large part of that region maintained the integrity of the borders rather well. However, in the south, the border between the United States and Mexico was frequently violated by Mexican nationals who sought work in the United States. For years before World War II, these border violations were tolerated since they allowed the influx of cheap labor for use in the bordering states for farm and ranch work. As their number increased, different laws were passed to permit a number to enter legally into this country for short periods of time. This was done, to make it possible to fill the vacancies that existed on those large agricultural enterprises which were not being filled by our own citizens. Some returned to Mexico voluntarily, others overstayed their time period and had to be rounded up and returned to their native country. Then there were others, that disappeared into the large cities and into other states, to make up the pool of illegal immigrants at large in this country. However, our border at that time was still, more or less a deterrent to the influx of a large number of illegal entries. Following World War II, a number of events took place that changed all this drastically.

First there was the slowly evolving liberal mentality that expounded the belief that we should right all the wrongs of the world. Inspired by such things as the poem on the base of the Statue of Liberty and backed by the philosophy of many liberals, who were well intentioned but misguided, a new ideology appeared on the American horizon. This ideology expressed the belief that all human beings in this world, who were in poverty or oppressed by a foreign nation should be allowed to find a refuge in this country. Furthermore, that we should favor those who had no education, no means of support, and lived in poverty, to enter first. That we should also shelter, feed, give medical aid, dress, educate and give rights of citizenship to these unfortunates. In addition, we should give them benefits from programs originally intended for, and paid for, by our citizens and its government. That they should also immediately receive benefits from programs which our own citizens must wait specific periods of time to be eligible for.

Secondly, a precedent was sent by our own government after the failure of the, "Bay Of Pigs," fiasco, in Castro ruled Cuba. Thousands of Cuban nationals were allowed to pour into south Florida, changing the complexion of that part of the state forever. This was followed in the 1970s, by the United States Government allowing the pouring of southeastern, "boat people," and

Vietnam nationals across our borders. These were blatantly simplified policies of immigration. No respect for our quota system, no physical examinations, no laboratory examinations, only a finely veiled pretense at showing that these people were invited here because of political rather than economic reasons. This then was the new criterion! A policy, that originated during the cold war, stating that those fleeing communism could defect to this country and be welcomed with open arms. At first the American people were jubilant and flattered that these people preferred Democracy over Communism, and believed that they should in some way be rewarded. We duped ourselves into thinking that this was valid evidence that our system was superior. All this led to the belief, by many of our citizens, that these were humanitarian efforts, and the ability of these dissidents to enter this country should have a different priority over our usual laws of immigration.

Finally, the great prosperity occurring in this country, countered by the extreme poverty and lack of work in Mexico, influenced many people south of the border to look toward the north for relief. Noting that the United States Government now was showing sympathy towards the unfortunates of the world, a laxness in enforcing the integrity of its borders, these foreign nationals were encouraged to pour across the border. They ignored our border patrols and the sovereignty of our nation, and thousands of Mexican nationals came illegally into this country. Our borders were violated and ignored, allowing our country to be invaded without even a shot being fired! They accomplished in this manner what no other foreign nation could dream of achieving with the force of arms. A nation that does not preserve the integrity of its borders cannot long exist as a sovereign nation. It becomes like a giant hemorrhage spurting out the life blood of this nation. Like a porous tent designed to keep out the harsh elements, now offering little resistance to those elements that it was designed to keep out.

Today in our country, there is little nationalistic fervor. many of our citizens, although they enjoy the fruits of a democratic society, do little to praise it. In fact they go out of their way to criticize their own government in favor of foreign doctrines, customs and grievances. Many go so far as to desecrate their own flag, in defense of other nation's opinions and actions, or in protest to their own country's policies and conduct. What has happened to the patriots of the past? Those who praised the accomplishments of their country, and who would protect its integrity with their very lives. Those whose credo was, "My country right or wrong, but my country."

Here we see another perversion of our liberties. The right to free thought and speech and opinion, used not to criticize political parties and our policies, but to use these instead to undermine our democratic processes and to champion the causes of other nations and political systems. The belief that they as citizens owe no allegiance to their own country, while at the same time enjoying all those freedoms which it provides for them. The same permissive ideology established by the liberal elements about us, which encourages our offspring to enjoy the fruits of their parent's labor, and at the same time condemning them as pawns in a restrictive establishment that conspires to force them to adhere to the rules of a civilized society.

Unlike the early immigrants of the turn of the century, these new ones do not come, to our country to be Americans. They come only for the political and economic benefits that they receive here. They are not interested in being absorbed into American society, nor its traditions or culture. They wish to merely live here, bringing with them their own institutions and culture. They do not even desire to adopt our language, but expect their adopted nation to provide for them the means to speak and read in their own language. They in essence desire to build a nation within a nation, preserving their culture and maintaining allegiance to their mother country. Many are not satisfied to be in this country themselves, but conspire to sneak across the border their families and relatives.

Meanwhile, those foreign nationals, who have obtained citizenship in this country, conspire with their countrymen to aid in their illegal entry. These naturalized forces have formed political groups and used our democratic institutions to help elect members of the legislation who will support their cause. They have in this way, with the support of a liberal press and political party, managed to subvert this government's attempt to preserve our borders and have managed to achieve for their illegal compatriots many government and state benefits. They have been successful in forming a political block so strong, that they have been able to lobby Washington and a number of state houses into providing bilingual teaching in schools and their language included in all public notices and regulatory signs. In addition, they have been successful in obtaining free medical treatment and other assistance for these illegal immigrants. What other nation on earth would provide for people who have broken their laws, not only freedom from prosecution, but free education, welfare and medical care.

They are also provided for under programs that our own citizens have paid for, and in which neither these illegals nor their country have contributed to. For those who cannot believe this is true, then please be informed that they are included for benefits under our own Social Security Disability Benefits program. Any of these illegal immigrants who are disabled, can apply for these benefits by merely reporting to the local Social Security Office and apply. They do not even have to pay for their own medical evaluation, this agency will pay for all necessary medical examinations, and in addition pay for a cab or other conveyances to bring them to the medical facilities, if they have no other means of transportation. Illegal immigrants are not punished for entering this country illegally, but are rewarded instead. These aliens from the South, who have never shed a drop of blood to win their freedom, who have never fought on foreign soil to defend and preserve it, now sneak or literally walk across our borders and are provided all the benefits that our citizens have paid, fought, worked and struggled for, just for the asking. In addition their country men, who are now naturalized citizens, not only encourage and support this illegal act, but make sure when they arrive that they are informed about all the benefits they can receive by just being here.

They are sure to accompany these aliens to the proper agencies, pointing out their rights and even interpreting for them since, they do not speak English. Whenever this government sets up barriers to stop this illegal entry, these illegals from the south vandalize them, tear them down or punch holes in them. Whenever the United State Government threatens to erect more substantial obstacles, string razor wire, or increase military and border patrols along the border, there is an outcry from the Latin communities and their liberal allies.

Lately, even the head of state of the country across our southern border, decried the use of military units to reinforce our determinations to keep illegals out as a military provocation. It has taken an economic crisis in the states burdened by the care of these aliens, to finally move our federal government to commit to a policy of preserving the integrity of our border to the south.

Although our southern border is the one that generates the greatest source of immigrants entering our country, the immigration of large numbers from other countries that enter legally, sanctioned arbitrarily by our country to help the politically persecuted, also has lead to many problems. The wholesale admission of Cuban, Oriental, and eastern European nationals, to compensate them for our failure to free them from their repressive governments, has also been a source of great problems for states and for citizens and commercial enterprises of these regions. This open immigration policy has not only brought personal and economic problems, but also danger to the health and welfare of the American citizens who have lived in these regions for many years. We are all familiar with the strife they have caused the fisherman in New England, the development of the Russian Mafia in the northeast, the Haitian and Colombian Gangs who run the narcotics trade in many of our large cities, the influx of thousands of Cubans into Florida, that has turned that area into a foreign country within our own borders. This country has enough homespun problem of its own, to go about importing more from outside its borders.

Orderly immigration under our quota system has mandated within it, a requirement that the applicants do not have contagious or communicable disease. No such requirement is enforced in our quotaless immigration, because of political reasons. This has allowed people with tuberculosis, intestinal parasites and other diseases, which are a threat to the health of the community, to enter this country. This has caused the incident of Pullmonary Tuberculosis, which had almost disappeared from this country 20 years ago, to greatly increase. New immigrants have been hired in the food industry with tape worms and other intestinal parasites, because of this government's failure to adhere to those provisions under our immigration laws, which were established to prevent these health threats to our citizens.

The first duty of any government is to protect its citizens from the intrusion into their lives by citizens of other nations. To admit some, in an orderly and a systematically regulated manner is one thing, to allow a mass influx of foreign nationals in a chaotic and unregulated manner poses a threat not only to its citizens, but to the nation as a whole.

One cannot argue with the Christian doctrine that we must help all our fellow human beings. However, not at the expense of disrupting our nation to the extent that states become bankrupt for their care, or our own citizens are threatened and our society and form of government undermined. If these illegal and legal immigrant grow in sufficient number that allows them to form a united front and elect representatives that look out only for their interest in detriment to the rest of the nation, then our nation will be fractionated. These immigrants do not champion the needs of the nation, but in the most part are interested in establishing the traditions and culture of the foreign nation from whence they came. Their prime aim is to further the interest of their society in the United States of America. They do not understand the concept of statehood. They look upon themselves as settlers in a new land where they can establish a new nation for themselves. And yet they do not mind accepting all the help and succor that its citizens enjoy.

As in any national or ethnic group, there are exceptions to these characterizations. However, problems are caused by the majority, not the few. The fact remains, that there are many immigrants in our country that in spite of being here for long periods of time, do not, and care not, to speak our native tongue. One cannot understand the culture, nor the concept of a democratic government unless they can first speak the tongue of their newly adopted country. One should not, nor be expected to abandon the traditions and culture of their mother country. However, any immigrant should learn the ways of the country in which they hope to spend the rest of their lives and rear their children. Those who are only looking for a place to live in, where their personal rights are guaranteed, and their bellies are always full, will never contribute much to its new society. For a nation to grow and flourish, the new immigrants must be assimilated into their society, this is the basis of multi-culturalism. This can never happen when those new citizens cannot speak the national language, and are so jealous and fixed into their own culture that they do not wish to be identified with those of others. This leads to ethnic enclaves, a condition which has led to conflict and discrimination for generations in the Old World.

Here we see the manipulation of laws that were passed to protect the citizens of this country from unrestricted foreign intrusion of citizens from foreign nations. The corrupting of those laws in turn also perverts the liberty we have been guaranteed to be free from foreign inundation. These laws have been changed arbitrarily by our government as tools for the use as foreign political policy, in detriment to health and welfare of the citizens of this country. If citizenship in the United States of America is so valueless that it can be obtained indiscriminately by anyone who desires it, then what foreign nation will respect the guarantees that the United States citizen engendered in the past.

Chapter XIII

Even those political practices not defined by our Constitution or the Bill of Rights, are perverted by our citizens. Such is the case of "lobbying." This is the practice of influencing government decisions by agents of special interests. The form of direct lobbying, is to exert pressure on the legislators, either State or Federal or both, by the use of publicity, compiled information, promotional campaigns, threat of political reprisals or pledges of support. These agents of lobbying groups may also apply indirect pressure, such as putting pressure on the legislature by using propaganda to create the impression of widespread popular support for an issue. Private interests have formed large powerful groups who spend large sums of money to influence the administration on existing legislation. These organizations are made up of large special interests groups, such as corporations, Labor, Education, Public Utilities, Farmers, Organized Medicine, Civil Rights, Environmental, Ad nauseam. Agents of these groups line the corridors of our Federal Government as well as many of the state houses across this nation. There have been many unethical as well as illegal interplay between legislators and agents of lobbying groups in the past. Some petty and some downright scandalous, as noted in the Lucuna Coat and Freezer incident during a Democratic administration in the late 1940s.

The Federal Government has passed a number of regulatory

laws to control lobbying through legislation. Two were created in the late 1940s and the latest in the early 1990s.

Lobbying seeks to put pressure on American Democracy and attempts to supplement geographic representation by a form of unofficial government. Any legislation passed by our government should be for the good of all the people, not in favor of any organized group. Lobbying has no place in a democratic form of government. It often is no better than political blackmail, or at best the purchase of favorable legislature by bribery. Bribery comes in many forms, much of it comes in a covert manner. Actual financial remuneration can be repaid in may devious ways, some methods are quite ingenious. Others in the form of promises and threats to enhance or diminish political advantages. Many a community has received lavish and outstanding public works and lucrative federal contracts, to pay back some legislator's favor to pass or suppress a piece of legislature. Others have been rewarded by plush jobs and important federal positions, as repayment for their cooperation with lobbing requests, from interest groups they had befriended years before. Our legislation should not put our welfare up for sale to the highest bidder.

The interests of any group or industry can be expressed in congressional committee hearings, in the light of public scrutiny where honest shortcomings can be expressed and rebuttals given. Many of our congressional and state legislative representatives are too beholding to these special interest groups to make honest decisions on legislation favoring or are deleterious to them. Our representatives should consider all their constituents when arriving at a decision, and not be forced to make them in repayment for some political or financial favors owed to special interests. Lobbying is corrupting to the democratic process, as evidenced in the scandals of other newer democratic countries. One of the most corrupting method of undermining any democratic process is bribing. It circumvents the legislating process by making enforcement of any regulation, or law, vulnerable to outside forces.

In many other governments, some even pretending to be democratic, the bribe is a way of life. By over regulating they can prolong or prevent many important functions among its citizens.

Those who wish to comply with them, must in essence purchase the legislature in order to have them enforced, others pay to have them circumvented. In many countries this system can create chaos, or makes it difficult to engage in foreign commerce. In many of these countries, citizens of other governments, including ours, are arrested under trumped up or petty charges, and then given outlandish jail sentences, causing their family and friends to pay large bribes for their release. Whether any government is corrupt or not, is very often measured by the integrity of its laws. The ability to maintain and enforce the laws and regulatory rules of a government is a hallmark of its stability.

Sometimes in this country, an entire administration can use lobbying methods to push ahead its own agenda. Again, any administration should adhere to the will of its people, rather than using intimidation or favors to gain support of legislators to pass some legislature which often has more to do with some ideology, rather than the welfare of all the people. This infraction of ethical government has been more notable in recent years. Behind the guise of Americanism, and supported by propaganda to enforce their claim of grass root support, they pass legislature contrary to the will of the people, and often in spite of their opposition. This type of legislation has caused much resentment between racial and other rights organizations, and has only succeeded in polarizing their views rather then arbitrating them. The support of any government for one group over another, as evidenced in many other countries, is froth with severe consequences. A Democracy is built upon the welfare of the majority, rather than the displeasure of an entire nation in order to cater to the few.

It is a sad commentary on our form of government, that a practice which has become an accepted part of our political system, and has no legislative basis for its existence, is so entrenched in the legislative process that its complete abolition has never been attempted nor demanded. These special interest groups are so powerful that they can influence the outcome of elections, and are feared by most politicians. Is this democracy? Is this government by the people? Is this government for the people? Is this what our forefathers envisioned when they were determined to form a type of government that could not be influenced by any out side forces, and to guarantee that this government would rule by the will of its people in order to form a more perfect union?

Whoever gave the right to these corrupters of the democratic process to intrude in the covenant between our elected representatives and the people? Why can they not be legislated out of existence? Why do not those citizens who are so intent upon their liberal agenda that they march and protest in the streets, do so for a practice that in reality threatens their democratic freedom more than abortion, gay rights, and animal abuse? If our representative only have ears for organized special groups, then who speaks for the average citizens who are suppose to be represented by those very people who cater to special interests. Who represents those citizens who are not black, not gay, have no real position on firearms; abortion is a moral issue which is and never will be a factor in their lives; who favor jobs and progress over environmental protection; do not feel that they wish their government to tell them what is dangerous to their health, feel that they have the intelligence and information to make their own decisions; can take care of their own religious needs; but expect those they elect to help provide them with freedom from oppression and the pursuit of happiness?

Perhaps our own representatives should take continued education courses in representative government, in order to refresh their memories of what their elected positions really mean! To let them know at the polls may take too long, they have too much time to make mischief in between. Legislation to regulate lobbying is only an exercise in futility. You will notice only regulation is mentioned. No where do you see an effort to stop their abuses. No one even mentions the possibility of abolishing this practice, or even better to outlaw the process all together! Can it be that political life without the aid of the goody givers would be unbearable?

Here we see that not only liberties can be perverted, but also political practices that have evolved with the passage of time and accepted as common practice. At its inception, lobbying seemed to be a logical method of informing the members of our legislative bodies about concerns that groups of citizens had in the passage of certain legislation which they wished to bring to their representatives. During some of our earlier administrations it had to do more with patronage and nepotism than with collective interests. At first, during our agrarian period, lobbying concerned itself mostly with the affairs of Agriculture. With the onset of the industrial revolution, then groups representing the railroads, the coal industry, and later the oil industry, made the legislative body aware of their concerns. For a while, captains of industry directly dealt with presidents and powerful elected officials. However, with the mandate to curtail the power of large industrial giants and the antitrust eras, it was finally found more prudent to let representatives of large industries lobby the legislators. This process was so successful, that lobbying as practiced today became an accepted part of the political system. The regulatory rules of the 1940s attempted to control lobbying through legislation. They required lobbyists to register and submit reports and financial statements, in addition they required many federal agencies to give notice of proposed rules to interested groups. More recent regulatory rules did little more than reinforce those already in existence, they did nothing to curtail their power or modify, let alone, abandon the practice. Here we see the Tyranny of the common man.

Even more threatening, is the power of creeping commercialism, which may in time corrupt the power of our own legislative processes in its effort to curtail the abuses of industry. Is it possible, that we may one day find that although we still maintained our political independence, that we have lost our economic freedoms?

CHAPTER XIV

The most alarming phenomena arising out of today's, permissive society, is lack of patriotism and the absence of a feeling of nationalism among many of our citizens, especially the younger generations. Before World War II to the period immediately after it, American Citizens were proud to be Americans and defended their government and their birthright both with words and with arms. We may have at times disagreed with some of our governments policies, but whenever Americans were in harms way, or other nations threatened us, our Allies, or our interests, Americans were proud to fight in defense of our country or its citizens. Young men would weep and be despondent if they were found physically unfit to enter the armed forces. During World War I and World War II young boys not of age to be taken into the service, would falsify documents and try all kinds of deceptions in order to be recruited or drafted into the Armed Forces.

Anyone speaking ill of our democratic way or desecrating our flag in public, would meet with speedy physical retaliation by others who heard and saw them. In spite of depressions, wars, and national disasters, Americans stood shoulder to shoulder in defense of their nation or neighbors. When their country called, all disagreements and animosities were put aside until the problem was resolved or victory was obtained. Some reading these words will say. "What corn," as if a show of patriotism is something to be ashamed of. These appear to be the same citizens who enjoy vulgarity, are in favor of all permissive liberalism, and have a cynical philosophy for anything American. At the same time, they are all too willing to reap the fruits of our democracy whose rights allows them to enjoy life and liberty, and the pursuit of happiness. They see no need to embrace or defend it, but are not reluctant to take advantage of those ideas that give them the right of free speech. They repay generations of Americans, who made it possible for them to live in a free society by their sacrifices, blood and dedication to the rule of the people, by attempting to tear down all its institutions and values, and even refusing to fight in its defense.

They invent all types of reasons to justify their cowardice, and their refusal to repay society for all the advantages they enjoy. As if that is not enough, many of these anti-American Americans pollute their bodies with addicting substances and contribute nothing to the society in which they live. Then when they have turned into the dregs of society, they are rehabilitated at the expense of those they despise, and when recovered, are embraced by the liberal elements and television talk shows as heroes who were able to, "shake the habit!" We speak of perversion! Here is true perversion! What could be more perverse than members of our society being praised and admired because they recovered from the results of their own intemperance, while vilifying their own government.

Then there are those who pervert the American tendency to have empathy for the unfortunates of the world. These individuals are so concerned about the plight and freedoms of others, that they forget about the welfare of their own country. They insist by public protest and the support of other liberal elements, for policies which while helpful to others would undermine or cause hardships to our own citizens and government. The United States cannot take in all the economically and politically depressed people of the world! Still, there are well intended, but misguided people in our country who insist that we should. As stated elsewhere in this text, if a millionaire decided that he would help as many people as he could, and gave a million people one dollar each. He would not make anyone rich, but in the process he would make himself poor.

This same philosophy holds true for our foreign aid. When the United States economy was strong, and Americans basked in their affluence and prosperity, to share their bountiful blessing with others not so fortunate people of the world, was proper. However, during this period of economic distress, and national budget deficits, the government should first be concerned with the welfare of its own people, before striving to bolster economies of other nations.

Here, we see the perversion of a national policy. At one time, the United States government, built on Christian ideas, was justified in helping others of the world in need. However, it was not a policy to be forever followed. Certainly it is not wrong for a nation, when they are prospering, to help others in need of assistance, by the same token, they should not be expected to do so during bad times. An economically depressed United States of America is not only bad for this country, but also for other nations who turn to us for assistance. It would behoove the world not to expect aid during our bad economic times, so that America can recover and be in a position sometime in the future to help them again. For if this nation loses its affluence and can never again be in a position to help others, then who will help the unfortunates of the world?

Our government has given away the wealth of our nation in acts of compassion and assistance to other nations ever since World War II. Starting with its, "Lend Lease policy," to Britain and Russia and after the war with its Marshall Plan. Taxes which were leveled against our citizens were not fully used for their benefit, instead large amounts were siphoned off to be used as a foreign policy tool to obtain the support of other nations, or governments. The same perverse programs that were followed at home, which believed that any problem could be solved by throwing money at it, was followed in our foreign aid policy. With the same results, in the same manner that large appropriations for education, welfare programs, medical care and many other problems were not solved by money in our own country, neither was our aid to other nations and governments beneficial to us. Much of it was stolen and misappropriated by their leaders and government and in return we only earned their disdain and hate.

We earned the unenviable distinction of a nation whose generosity was gladly accepted, and then told to go home. "Yankee Go Home," is a phrase still found written on walls of many of the countries we have defended and benefited. Others that we have lent money to never repaid us, and a generous United States of America canceled their debts. In those countries where American aid rebuilt these nations after World War II, in spite of the fact that they were our enemies, they recovered and in time became our greatest economic competitors. We built up these nations so that they would not become communistic and in return, they did so well under a democratic government and with our aid that they became major players in the game of world commercialism.

This is a familiar scenario in which the teacher is out done by its pupil. That wealth, which belonged rightfully to the American people, was given away to and squandered on, other nations. Nations that not only did not appreciate it, but resented our very presence in their country. That wealth, which should have been used to preserve our infra-structures and produce great public works and improvements, went instead into the pockets of foreign politicians and governments, for which we got nothing in return but ingratitude. This attitude of hooray for everybody else, but to hell with our own nation, is a perversion of our entire Democratic process. Are we becoming a nation of too many politicians and too few patriots?

Here we see the perversion of an American policy. Foreign aid given without restraint and for purposes contrary to the good of our country. A worthwhile policy that was liberalized and extended to the point that it no longer produced the result for which it was originally intended.

Chapter XV

Will the greatest experiment since the beginning of time, in the creation of a true democratic society, falter? Will the United States of America join the other great governmental experiments which did not stand the test of time, and be thrown into the scrap heap of failed good intentions? Has this great nation which was the most powerful, independent, compassionate, freedom loving, generous, non-threatening society on earth reached its zenith, and is now declining. Can it be possible, that so noble an idea will only survive for just over 200 years. Will it finally prove that common men and women, when they are asked to rule themselves, will eventually develop a tyranny of their own? Is it possible that the origin of this tyranny is the result of the perversion of our own liberties? If the rule by one creates tyranny and the rule by many also produces a tyranny of its own, then what will finally be the fate of mankind?

Can it be, that although the cause of the demise of other great nations was usually the result of devious and unscrupulous acts that in contrast, the United States of America will fail as a result of the lack of common sense? That in the end, we will find that our nation was guided by illogical people who made illogical decisions, and will be the first great nation which will fall, because of emotional, immature, and illogical determinations. That many of the decisions that were made by our own people were not wise, did not make any sense, and can in no way be regarded as intelligent. Many of our major premises are flawed and emotional expressions, instead of well thought out concepts, hammered out on the table of common sense and logic.

The proof of the pudding is in its eating. What has been the result of the perversion of our liberties? Has the over permissive rearing of our children produced very desirable adults? Are our cities still citadels of cleanliness, beauty and order? Are we still a moral, God fearing people? Has our music, art and literature reached the heights of perfection? Are our children better educated, and go to schools and colleges that are well disciplined, with an abundance of good teachers and subjects to learn? Do they speak and read well? Do they read literature and see great works of literature and art on the silver and television screens? Are our streets safe and devoid of crime, and our courts able to dispense with the unlawful speedily and with judicial dignity? Are our people God fearing and law abiding, and free from intemperance and bad habits? Are our family units in tact and functioning in a manner to be envied by the rest of the world? Is the great gift of free speech being used to disseminate news, and the mainstay of this country's watch dog? Are we still a moral nation, protecting the innocent and shunning those who would defile our sensibilities? If the answer to many of these questions is NO! Then the perversion of our liberties has not benefited this nation. Those who demand that we stay on the same course regardless of its results, they then are the new tyrants. They create fear, immorality, loss of religious beliefs, burdensome taxes, death and injustice, as the tyrants of old. Finally, we have become our own tyrants!

A society in which there is no legal or religious deterrent, is one that is in chaos. Discipline is the keystone of a civilized community. The deterrent which is provided by fear of punishment in this present world, or an after life, is the basic motivation for the discipline of many members of man and woman kind. This is what awakens man's moral conscious and allows those qualities in him, which are also embedded in his make-up to come to the fore and squelch those urges which are antisocial. Over permissiveness and perverted liberties only foster the tyranny which lies within all of us. The misguided belief of many Americans, that if a freedom is good for you more of it should be better is as erroneous in maintaining a civilized society, as it is in the field of medicine. It is difficult for many in our nation to understand that if liberty is good, that unrestrained freedom is not better. It is foreign to the concept of a free democracy to believe that unrestrained freedom leads to perversion of our liberties, and the disruption of the democratic process. Total freedom means absence of all restraints. If this philosophy is used as a method of raising a new generation, starting at childhood with complete permissiveness, and reinforcing this concept during the rebellious years by the absence of repression, and then finally encouraging the abandonment of all religious and legal deterrents, then we have a totally undisciplined individual. If this philosophy were to be universally followed, then we will have a totally undisciplined society. Such a condition would produce a chaotic community which will change a civilized society into a state of barbarism.

CHAPTER XVI

While we in the United States of America have been guarding against communism and the loss of our political freedoms, creeping in without our notice is an even bigger threat, commercialism. Insidiously, but relentlessly corporative America is taking away our economic freedoms. One lesson we have learned from the aftermath of World War II, is that its easier and more profitable to defeat an adversary by economic means than by force of arms. The aim of any conquest, is the economic rewards that one country achieves over its adversaries when they defeat them. This, however, is a destructive process, both in human life, and to the physical assets of a nation. In modern warfare, with its highly destructive weapons, the victorious nation wins only a pile of rubbish, and a demolition of some of its own assets. The end result of World War II has taught many nations that its far better to compete with other nations economically than by force of arms. What Germany and Japan could not achieve with their mighty war machines, they accomplished by economic competition. They did not have to conquer parts of our nation, all they had to do was buy them! These facts should teach us all a lesson, the power of commercialism as used in a capitalistic democracy is awesome!

Our nation started as a free society, unshackled from the restrictions of the Old World. We not only had political freedom, but were able to exercise our rights in a free marketplace. Unfortunately, our forefathers were so focused on our personal freedoms that they never even considered that our economic freedoms should also be protected. They never considered that political freedom and capitalism were two sides of the same coin. They believed that democracy and a free marketplace could live side by side, one enhancing the other.

At the beginning, in the newly created United States of America, commerce was composed of farming, livestock and small shops: bakery, shoemakers, groceries, butchers, drug stores, etc. Then there were also services: livery stables, barbers, domestics, teamsters, etc. and crafts: carpenters, masons, wheelwrights, wagon and coachwright, etc. and all the tools and materials necessary to perform these functions. These commercial arrangements were maintained until the industrial revolution. The coming of the railroad and the industrialization of America, brought many changes in the world of commerce. Industries which started as family efforts soon found advantages in creating corporations. Those that did not, often were unable to meet their competition and were sold or taken over by other corporations. The need for coal, and finally oil, to turn the engines of industry and run the trains to bring this source of energy to them, soon made the oil and coal industries a mighty industrial force in our country.

The creation of the assembly line concept, by men like Henry Ford and others, soon made products of need and luxury available to the American public at affordable prices. These corporations, with their control of labor, cheap energy and material, soon became industrial giants. The heads of these corporations very often abused their positions and exploited others, and many were more powerful than some monarchies. The men who owned or managed these industries, such as J.P. Morgan soon became enormously rich and attained great political power in this country. The excesses in their wealth and life style can even today be seen in the large mansions and manicured gardens of the Hearsts, Vanderbilts, DuPonts and others, which are now open to the public. Like great potentates of old, they ruled their industrial empires with a tight fist.

Their corporate excesses, however, became so great, that an anti-trust era ensued, which reigned in some of their more flagrant abuses by the creation of anti-trust laws and other laws to curb unfair practices. It took the creation of labor unions, the great labor turmoil of the 1930s, and the leverage created by World War II, to finally free labor from the brutal abuses of management. After a period of prosperity and labor and management truces, the excesses of labor and the opening up of an independent world economy, corporative America once again got the upper hand. Presently, instead of the big boss owned corporations of the past, the tax laws now make it more profitable for the captains of industry to legally structure their corporations, with large blocks of stocks and a chief executive officer at its head. All this finally set the stage for the commercial take-over of America.

In the 1940s immediately after that great war, except for the large smokestack industries, much of the American Market place was made up of small shops, much in the same manner that England still has maintained to this day. Except for the large department stores which occupied the downtown sections of the cities and towns, most of personal shopping was done at the local stores. Everyone shopped at their favorite butcher shop, grocery store, baker, fresh produce store etc. Bread, milk, butter and eggs were items which could be delivered to the house, if one preferred. Those of a past generation, can still remember the reassuring sounds of the rattling of bottles and the horse shoes hitting the roadways, very early every morning when milk was delivered. There were a few chain stores such as the A&P and Acme stores, but in many neighborhoods they were like the convenience stores of today. Many people preferred fresh food items at their own local stores. In some locations they did well, but in others, especially in ethnic neighborhoods, they were shunned.

After World War II, corporate America looked about for other markets into which investment of capital would gain greater returns. At that same time, some entrepreneurs were experimenting with omnibus stores. Some corporations had faith in this concept, and using the old adage, "everyone has to eat," created the supermarket. They would create stores in which all food items would be sold. It would be a one shopping adventure, where meat, fresh vegetables, deserts, breads and canned foods, grains and dairy products could all be purchased in one store. In addition, they had the foresight to anticipate that the automobile would become the prime mode of transportation in the years ahead. Therefore, they put the store at one end, and surrounded it with parking areas.

As in other industries they also were aware that products would be cheaper if they bought them in tremendously large amounts. With the constant improvement in refrigeration as a result of the war effort, they felt that they could store large amounts of perishable food items with little spoilage. Putting these factors together, they created supermarkets in choice locations in the areas with which they were familiar. They had grand openings, with members of the entertainment world, sport figures, or local politicians part of the opening ceremonies. With unheard of low prices on many items, they seemed to be an instant success. There were large crowds on opening day, who were agog at the large shiny modern interiors and the variety of food stuff. At first many people kept their allegiance with their local food shops. However, once they recognized the values and the carnival like atmosphere at these newly created stores, they soon deserted them for the super market. As the post war years brought increasingly more automobile traffic to city streets, the inability to park near the small shops, influenced many advocates of the these shops to abandon them.

Finally, the smaller shops found they could not compete with the prices and variety of the super markets, this tolled the knell for small independent shops. Many of the shopkeepers welcomed the coming of omnibus food stores. Bakers did not have to get up early in the morning to bake bread. They could work in the large corporate bakeries, where the use of preservatives and special baking and storage procedures did not make it necessary for them to arise early. Also, their hours were defined and not affected financially by changes in price of baking materials, wastage, or fluctuations in the economy. In addition, they were guaranteed vacation and sick leave, something which very few had in the past. The same was true of other merchants, the butchers went to work at the super markets, and so did the grocers, the butter and egg men, and many others. In the beginning, it appeared that this concept of shopping would be a boone to the food industry and the public. This concept opened up avenues to other enterprises; contract purchasing with farmers, ranchers and dairy farmers; the building of large storage structures and refrigerated ware-houses to store and preserve the large purchases by the food industry. As these corporations expanded, they found it more profitable to purchase their own fleet of trucks and hire drivers to ship the merchandise to their stores.

In time, the food corporations had put most of the small food stores out of business. As it is true in nature, that the large fish eat the small ones, so it is in corporate America. In this manner, the food industry was born. Not an industry made up of free independent owners, but as employees under the control of their bosses. The small food stores owners traded their independence for industrial benefits, a trade they would later learn to regret.

In the next 30 years this same scenario was repeated by corporations as they took over other parts of the American market. The same was done in the hardware business, the automobile servicing business, luncheon and hamburger establishments, drug stores and infinitum.

Today there are few small businesses and shops remaining. Some stores banded together to form associations so that they could also have the advantage of large purchases and cheaper prices. However, many found that they still could not compete with the large corporations who were willing to lose money on a few lead items, so that they could make up the loss on large rapid turn-over sales. These either sold out to the corporations or formed one of their own. In time, either by buy-outs or hostile take-overs, many of these markets eventually fell into the hands of just a few large corporations.

Once a market was dominated by a few giant corporations, then the fun was over for their employees and the public, for they felt little loyalty towards either. The bottom line for any of these industries was profit! Suddenly, prices increased on all food products and the employees were faced with long hours and short pay. Now the shop keepers found out too late the price they paid for their leisure. One blessing of freedom was independence, not only political, but occupational freedom with a free marketplace. A major reason why many people were shopkeepers was because as such they were their own bosses. Many immigrants remembered the abuse they took from harsh managers of stores and industries in the Old Countries, and sought to avoid working for others in their newly adopted nation. These store owners never gave into the corporations, and some are still in existence today, and are called, "Mom and Pop," stores, since they are all elderly people. The next generation, not endowed with the Old World work ethics, were easy marks for the corporations. The public, as is so often the case, was a big loser. Now they paid higher prices for many prepared and frozen products, that they could once buy fresh at a much cheaper price. The small shopkeepers frequently went to local produce markets and purchased meat, vegetables and fresh fish which had just arrived from farms and fishing boats. Now in the supermarkets, what was called fresh, was frozen and shipped from a distance, full of additives such as sodium nitrite or sulfites as preservatives, and thawed out just before sold. Meat which was at one time purchased from the local farms or via the slaughter houses, now took long trips in refrigerated cars from other parts of the country or the world. The old timers tasted the difference, but newer generations accustom to the taste never knew any better.

The abuses of labor by management in the food industry, resulted in the unionization of the food workers. Once in power, union demands made food prices even more expensive.

In this writing, the food industry take over is used as a model of how corporate America can take over any market and turn free independent workers into vessels of industry. These men and women still have their political freedoms, but have lost their economic independence. This is creeping commercialism! It is bad enough when this happens in the food and commodities market, but when it occurs in the health field, then we are all in jeopardy!

In the same manner in which it has occurred in the food industry, there are very few fields over which the large corporations in America have not gained economic control. There are few independent businesses or shops left in our country. Unless something occurs to stop this process, gradually all Americans will have to work for someone else.

At first, labor was able to reverse much of the abuse of management, unfortunately the unions finally began to abuse their own powers. This eventually lead to their own demise. With an available and cheap foreign labor markets, unions have lost any leverage that they had over management. Now corporate America has it all! Unfortunately, the increase in profits that industry earns as a result of curtailment of labor costs and the cheaper foreign material and services, is never passed on to the public. It is distributed to the share holders, business expansion projects, upper management and the chief executive Officers. The public is always told that prices do not come down because of inflation, increase in the cost of materials, the price of doing business and repressive taxation. No one ever questions why prices do not come down when we have none or little inflation; prices on raw material and energy moderate; and when taxes beneficial to corporate America is passed.

Presently these corporations are in the process of taking over the health field. They package medical care like any commodity and try to sell it on the open market like so many cans of beans. In collusion with them is the medical profession and the pharmaceutical industries. The medical field flitted with the commercial aspect of medical care for years, like some giant moth to a flame and finally has been consumed by them. Medicine is now no longer a profession, but a giant multiple billion dollar business.

If the danger of the commercialism of America stopped here, it would be bad enough. Now in addition, we are faced with the interplay and collusion between these different corporations. Endangering not only our economic freedoms, but the health and welfare of the entire nation as well. If eventually there are no more independent workers in the United States, neither in the professions, nor industry, nor the arts, nor any facet of human occupation, then we will all be employees. The result would be, that if anyone lost their job, they would also lose their medical benefits, their dental benefits, Pharmacy benefits, and whatever benefits can be acquired by being an employee. In this event, one may ask, "Why then does not the unemployed individuals pay for these services themselves when no longer in a prepaid plan?" The answer is, that unless one is independently wealthy, no one can afford the price of these services today. There seems to be an unwritten law that when a corporation takes over an independent service or business, frequently the price for this service suddenly becomes so exorbitant, that only a prepaid plan can pay for it. This may be because, when a corporation makes an obscene amount of money, devices must be found to spend it all. In addition, industrial bureaucracy has become as bad as governmental bureaucracy. The simplest of business or profession must be complicated by forms, computers, word processors, expensive communication systems, and the people to run them. An example is the medical business. When it was a profession, doctors could see a large number of patients with a secretary and one nurse. Now one cannot go to a medical or dental facility without seeing a myriad of workers, mostly women, milling around in white uniforms. One is a receptionist; one gets your records and weighs you; another takes your blood pressure, pulse and temperature; another escorts you to an examining room where another assists the doctors. Today the entire medical business has been turned into a managed care program. What this means, is that this health organization is more interested in managing the cost of your treatment, than your health. The same can be said of the dental profession, although it has not yet become a business, it is well on its way.

The Pharmacy profession has met with the same fate. The corner drugstore with the pharmacist, who was for many years, the first tier of medical treatment, has long ago been taken over by corporate America. Stripped of its professionalism, its now relegated to the back of super markets, or to a small space in the back of novelties, sundries and cosmetics.

These examples present a frightening possibility for the eventual total loss of economic freedom in this country. If we someday find that we all are employees, and its impossible to live in our country without employment, what good is our political freedoms? Will it someday, come to pass that we must have insurance for every facet of our lives? That we will have food insurance, energy insurance, gasoline insurance, rent insurance and funeral insurance. Which will mean that we will get only walking around money for our pay, while the remainder of our salaries will be used to pay the premiums on all of our insurances. Is it then not possible, that until retirement, a loss of employment will mean total destitution for the entire family? If this occurs, then we will again be in the grip of overseers, who will have the power to control our economic welfare. What then will our political freedoms mean to us? Democracy without a full stomach will never lead to the fulfillment of happiness, pursuit, yes, acquisition, no?

Do not think that these prophesies are far fetched, for if you examine the evidence, we are already moving in that direction. Perhaps, if democracy fails, as in the case of socialism and communism, then commercialism may take their place as the new tyranny against man and woman kind. Beware America! A new tyranny is threatening you! Keep a vigil over the commercialism creeping toward you, for that is your new enemy!

Printed in the USA
CPSIA information can be obtained
at www.ICGtesting.com
JSHW022337140824
68134JS00019B/1541

9 781681 621548